Collins Primary Maths
Pupil Book 3

6

Series Editor: Peter Clarke

Authors: Andrew Edmondson, Elizabeth Jurgensen,
Jeanette Mumford, Sandra Roberts

Contents

Shape and space: (reflective symmetry, reflection and translation)/Reasoning and generalising about shapes	To recognise where a shape will be after reflection in a mirror line touching the shape at a point (sides of shape not necessarily parallel or perpendicular to the mirror line)	66–67, 68–69
	To recognise where a shape will be after reflection in two mirror lines at right angles (sides of shape all parallel or perpendicular to the mirror line)	70–71
	To make and investigate a general statement about familiar shapes by finding examples that satisfy it	72–73, 82–83, 84–85
	To consolidate work on translations and rotations	74–75, 76–77, 78–79, 80–81
Measures: (time)/ Problems involving measures (time)	To identify and use appropriate operations (including combinations of operations) to solve word problems involving numbers and quantities based on measures (time), using one or more steps	86–87
Measures: (length)/Making decisions	To use, read and write standard metric units of length (l, ml), including their abbreviations and relationships between them	88–89
	To convert smaller to larger units (ml, l) and vice versa	90–91
	To know imperial units (pint, gallon)	92–93
	To know rough equivalents of litres and pints or gallons	92–93
Problems involving measures (capacity)	To identify and use appropriate operations (including combinations of operations) to solve word problems involving numbers and quantities based on measures (capacity), using one or more steps	94–95
Mental calculation strategies (+ and −)	To use known number facts and place value to consolidate mental addition/subtraction: for all numbers to 20	96–97, 98–99
	To extend written methods to column addition/subtraction of numbers involving decimals	96–97, 98–99
	To add or subtract any two-digit numbers, including crossing 100; derive sums and differences	100–101
	To derive quickly decimals that total 0·1 or 1 or 10; add several numbers	102–103
Properties of numbers and number sequences	To count on in steps of 0·1, 0·2, 0·25, 0·5... and then back	106–107
	To recognise prime numbers to at least 20	108–109
	To factorise numbers to 100 into prime factors	108–109
	To make and investigate a general statement about familiar numbers by finding examples that satisfy it	110–111
Reasoning and generalising about numbers	To develop from explaining a generalised relationship in words to expressing it in a formula using letters as symbols	112–113, 114–115

Moving places

Practice

1 Find the number that matches the description.

7 509 247	9 651 977	4 310 556
5 299 738	2 123 431	6 684 937
5 821 800	9 452 549	5 000 200

    a The hundreds digit and the hundred thousands digit are the same.
    b The units digit is the highest digit in the number.
    c The ten thousands digit is zero.
    d The millions digit is one higher than the units digit.
    e If the number was written out backwards it would be the same.

2 Choose three of the numbers and write them out in words.

3 Work out these calculations.

a $496 \times 10 =$ ⬚

b $2872 \times 100 =$ ⬚

c $687 \div 10 =$ ⬚

d $3460 \div 100 =$ ⬚

e $96 \cdot 7 \times 10 =$ ⬚

f $58703 \div 100 =$ ⬚

g $4872 \times$ ⬚ $= 487200$

h $586 \div$ ⬚ $= 5 \cdot 86$

i ⬚ $\times 10 = 9760$

j ⬚ $\div 100 = 28 \cdot 7$

k ⬚ $\times 100 = 970000$

l $62 \cdot 8 \times$ ⬚ $= 6280$

m $27400 \div$ ⬚ $= 274$

n $68700 \div$ ⬚ $= 6 \cdot 87$

o ⬚ $\div 100 = 0 \cdot 06$

p ⬚ $\times 100 = 520$

q $9731 \div$ ⬚ $= 97 \cdot 31$

r $84 \div$ ⬚ $= 0 \cdot 84$

s ⬚ $\times 10 = 87000$

t ⬚ $\div 10 = 930000$

u $72863 \times$ ⬚ $= 728630$

v ⬚ $\div 100 = 569 \cdot 2$

w $572 \div$ ⬚ $= 5 \cdot 72$

x ⬚ $\times 100 = 482$

y ⬚ $\times 10 = 3$

Refresher

1 Copy out each number and write what the red digit represents.

   a 52366   b 47210   c 96547

   d 75321   e 632655   f 128075

   g 647321   h 7526395   i 8632150

2 Write out these last two numbers in words.

3 Work out the multiplication calculations.

   a 28×10 b 45×10 c 286×100 d 173×10 e 4862×100

   f 7982×10 g 4.7×10 h 3.12×100 i 5.32×10 j 9.67×100

4 Work out these division calculations.

   a $9100 \div 10$ b $7280 \div 10$ c $1700 \div 100$ d $300 \div 100$ e $438000 \div 100$

   f $58700 \div 10$ g $970 \div 100$ h $45 \div 10$ i $1273 \div 100$ j $15.6 \div 10$

Challenge

a My garden is 45 m long. How many pieces of turf will I need if they are each 45 cm long?

b The shop orders 12 800 packs of coloured pencils.
   In each pack there are 10 pencils.
   The packs are in boxes of 100.
   How many pencils are there?
   How many boxes will they arrive in?

c A suitcase weighs 45·6 kg. What is one hundredth of the weight in g?

What's the arrow?

Practice

1 Round these numbers to the nearest multiple of 10, 100 and 1000.

   a 452 386   b 171 361   c 649 225   d 100 505   e 643 849

   f 7 638 196   g 8 632 482   h 9 158 219   i 2 633 501   j 6 348 222

2 Estimate the whole number or decimal marked by each arrow.

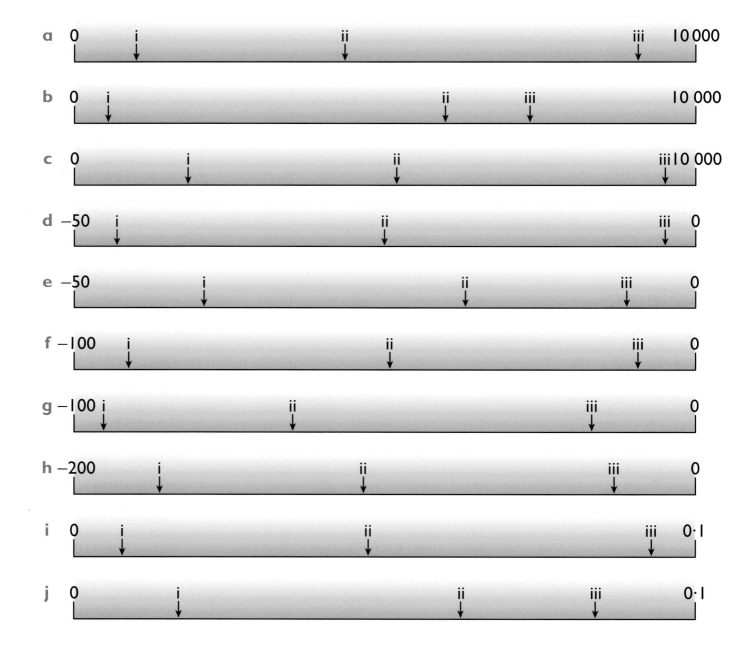

Example
572 → 570 → 600

Refresher

1 Round these numbers to the nearest multiple of 10 and 100.

   a 652   b 821   c 479   d 551   e 368

   f 3612   g 4551   h 7929   i 76824   j 91362

2 Estimate the whole number or decimal marked by each arrow.

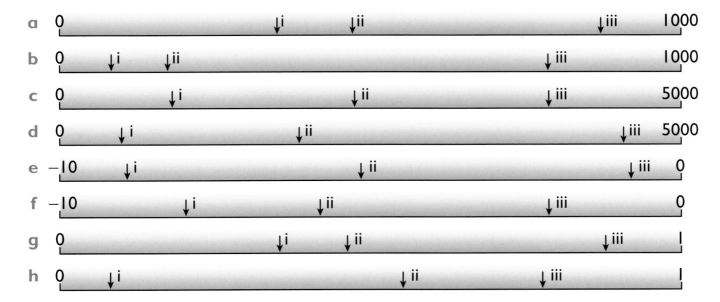

Challenge

1 Estimate the whole number or decimal marked by each arrow.

   a 0 ..... ↓i ..... ↓ii ..... ↓iii 1000

   b 0·06 ..... ↓i ..... ↓ii ..... ↓iii ..... 0·07

   c 1·76 ..... ↓i ..... ↓ii ..... ↓iii ..... 1·77

   d 2·51 ..... ↓i ..... ↓ii ..... ↓iii ..... 2·52

2 Explain how you worked out your estimates.

7

Estimate it

Practice

Work out your estimates. Show how you have worked out each one.
You can use a calculator.

1 Estimate what fraction of each cake has been eaten.

a   b   c   d

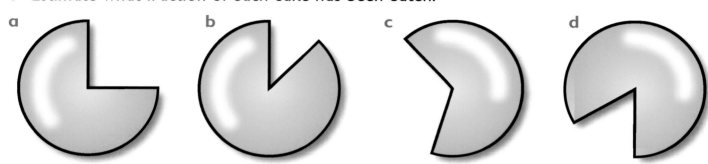

2 Estimate what fraction of the bottles are full.

a   b   c   d

3 Draw a line 15 cm long to represent these ropes. Show where to cut off these fractions.

a $\frac{2}{10}$

b $\frac{3}{8}$

c $\frac{3}{5}$

d $\frac{7}{15}$

4 Estimate how many 1p coins will make a line 1 km long.

5 Estimate how many loaves of bread you will eat in a year.

6 Estimate how many fingers and thumbs there are in your school.

7 Estimate how many hours you sleep in a year.

8 Estimate how many words there are in the book you are reading.

Refresher

1 Order these sets of numbers from smallest to largest.

   a −6, −78, 2, 0, 63, −10   b −25, 25, 2, 5, −5, −52
   c −100, 59, −58, 105, −7, 49   d 12, −23, 72, −101, 85, −48
   e 100, −1, −7, 86, −72, −51, 73

2 Estimate how many slices of bread you eat in a month.

3 Estimate how many hours of television you watch in a month.

4 Estimate how many hours you sleep in a month.

5 Estimate how many eyes there are in your school.

Challenge

1 Estimate how many entries there are in a telephone directory.
2 Estimate the height of everyone in your school standing on each other's shoulders.

Rounding remainders

Practice

Read each story.

Write the division calculation and answer.

If there is a remainder, think carefully whether you need to round your answer **up** or **down**.

a The school has raised £560 for a number of pupils to attend the ballet. Tickets cost £6 each. How many pupils can attend?

b 776 people attend the mid-week matinée performance of *Swan Lake*. Each row of seats fits 9 people. How many rows are needed?

c 195 people have asked to sit in a Balcony Box seat. Each box seats 6 people. How many boxes are needed?

d The Ballet Company takes £546 on souvenir brochures in one evening. Each brochure costs £7. How many did the Company sell?

e 772 people have tickets along one side of the balcony. Seats are in rows of 8. How many rows can be filled?

f Sandwiches are sold in packs of 4 during the interval. The kitchen has made 382 sandwiches. How many packs can be made up?

Refresher

Look at the numbers below.

1 Find the multiple shown on the top cube that comes **before** each number.

2 Find the multiple shown on the top cube that comes **after** each number.

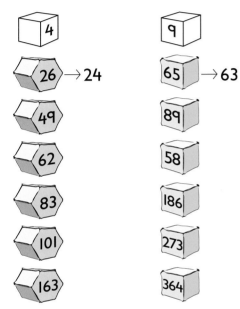

4

26 → 24
49
62
83
101
163

9

65 → 63
89
58
186
273
364

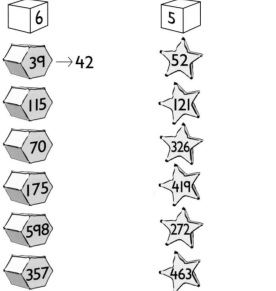

6

39 → 42
115
70
175
598
357

5

52
121
326
419
272
463

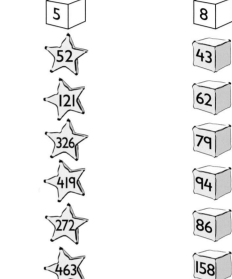

8

43
62
79
94
86
158

Challenge

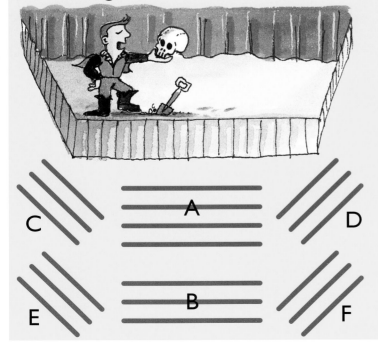

C
A
E
B
D
F

Information

Number of seats per row in each block.

A → 9   C and D → 7
B → 8   E and F → 6

Write your own word problems that involve rounding the answer up (↑) or down (↓) for each of the calculations below.

Use the information on this page and in the Practice activity.

a 652 ÷ 8 ↑   b 656 ÷ 7 ↑

c 384 ÷ 9 ↓   d 572 ÷ 6 ↓

Revising multiplication and division

Practice

1 Find the total cost of purchasing these items in pounds.

Write the calculation and answer. Work out the answer mentally.

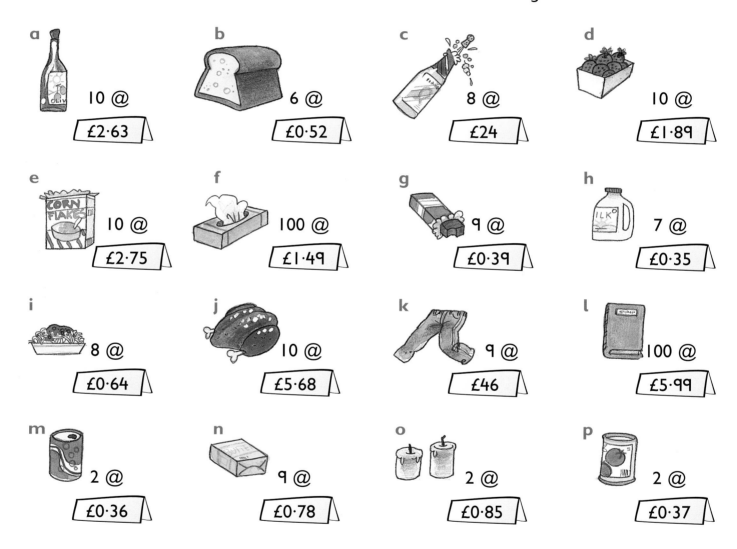

a 10 @ £2·63

b 6 @ £0·52

c 8 @ £24

d 10 @ £1·89

e 10 @ £2·75

f 100 @ £1·49

g 9 @ £0·39

h 7 @ £0·35

i 8 @ £0·64

j 10 @ £5·68

k 9 @ £46

l 100 @ £5·99

m 2 @ £0·36

n 9 @ £0·78

o 2 @ £0·85

p 2 @ £0·37

2 Look at the total cost. How much did it cost per item?

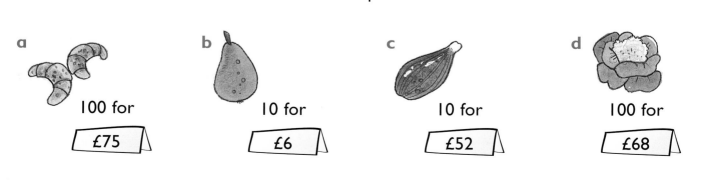

a 100 for £75

b 10 for £6

c 10 for £52

d 100 for £68

Refresher

The Supermarket is having problems with one of its cash registers.

Some of the totals for each item are incorrect. Find the incorrect totals.

Write the calculation and the correct answer.

SUPERMARKET

	£
Tin soup 4@ 0·52	2·80
Breakfast cereal 10@ 1·84	18·40
Champagne 3@ 24·00	75·00
Bread 9@ 0·46	4·60
Bottle drink 10@ 1·52	15·02
Chicken 10@ 4·24	42·40

SUPERMARKET

	£
Mini B-B-Q 3@ 53·00	153·00
Margarine 5@ 0·65	3·15
Spaghetti 6@ 0·49	4·90
Tin tomatoes 100@ 0·09	0·90
Milk 2@ 0·36	72·20
Olive oil 10@ 3·73	37·30
Washing powder 10@ 4·82	48·00

Challenge

Three children played a place value game.

They recorded their work on a place value chart.

They wrote their starter number on the chart.

They then turned over operation cards and recorded the answers
until they reached their final score.

Example

● 50

	Th	H	T	U	·tth	hth
Start→				·	5	0
×10			5	· 0	0	
×2		1	0	· 0	0	
×9		9	0	· 0	0	

Final score→						

Find out who had the highest score.

Record your work on a place value chart.

Start number

Child 1

9 → ×12 ÷10 ×2 ×10 ÷4 ×25 ÷100 ÷10 ×8

Child 2

·60 → ×2 ×6 ×10 ×50 ÷100 ×15 ÷100 ×6 ÷10

Child 3

52 → ×50 ÷100 ×12 ÷10 ×4 ÷100 ×2 ×100 ÷3

13

Multiplication methods

Practice

1 Approximate the answer to each calculation.

a 254×13

b 342×23

c 457×25

d 467×14

e 236×28

f 368×47

g 263×35

h 176×38

i 219×64

j 842×19

k 194×86

l 624×27

2 For each of the calculations above, use the grid method to work out the answer. Match the answer to its calculation to check if your working is correct.

Example
376×18

×	300	70	6	
10	3000	700	60	3760
8	2400	560	48	+3008
				6768

11 425   6688   9205

16 684   17 296   3302

14 016   6608   16 848

7866   6538   15 998

Refresher

1 Partition each of these numbers.

Example
$376 \rightarrow 300 + 70 + 6$

a 274   b 368
c 412   d 657
e 810   f 403
g 629   h 532
i 195   j 711
k 205   l 350

2 Round each number to the nearest multiple of 10 and multiple of 100.

Example
$376 \rightarrow 380, 400$

a 452   b 638
c 327   d 424
e 710   f 569
g 271   h 183
i 606   j 595

Challenge

For each question, use the grid method to work out the missing digit.

Example

$164 \times 1\boxed{2} = 1968$

$\times$	100	60	4
10	1000	600	40
2	200	120	8

$$1640$$
$$+ \ 328$$
$$\overline{1968}$$

a $2\boxed{}7 \times 25 = 5675$
b $326 \times 1\boxed{} = 4564$
c $\boxed{}38 \times 22 = 9636$
d $59\boxed{} \times 25 = 14775$
e $374 \times \boxed{}4 = 8976$

f $1\boxed{}9 \times 33 = 5577$
g $12\boxed{} \times 48 = 6000$
h $462 \times 1\boxed{} = 6930$
i $\boxed{}34 \times 34 = 21556$
j $716 \times 1\boxed{} = 13604$

Multiplication methods

Practice

1 Write multiplication facts for each box of numbers.

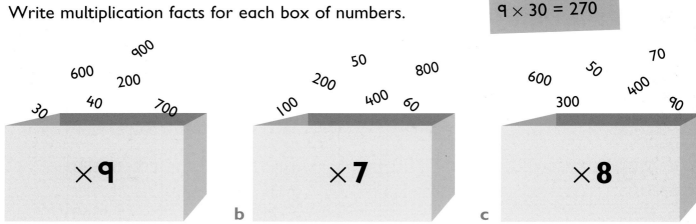

a   ×9

900
600   200
40   700
30

b   ×7

50   800
200   400
100   60

c   ×8

70
600   50   400
300   90

2 Approximate the answer first. Use the standard method of recording to work out the answer to each calculation.

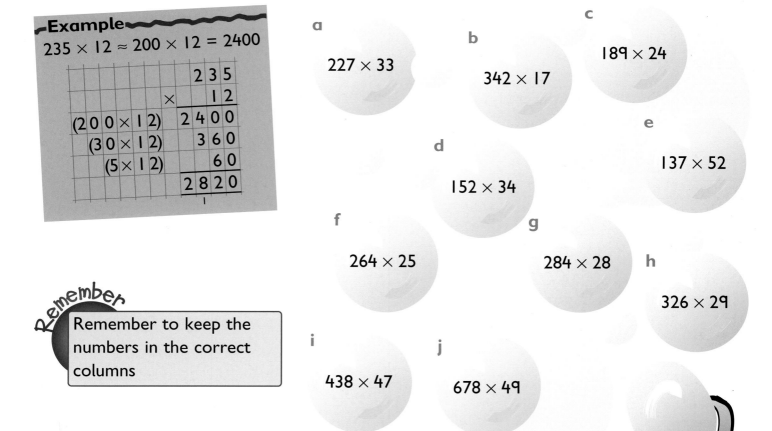

Example

235 × 12 ≈ 200 × 12 = 2400

```
                 2 3 5
          ×        1 2
(200×12)    2 4 0 0
 (30×12)      3 6 0
  (5×12)         6 0
            2 8 2 0
                1
```

a 227 × 33

b 342 × 17

c 189 × 24

d 152 × 34

e 137 × 52

f 264 × 25

g 284 × 28

h 326 × 29

i 438 × 47

j 678 × 49

Remember

Remember to keep the numbers in the correct columns

Refresher

Choose five calculations. Approximate the answer first, then use the grid method to work out the answer.

a 176×13

b 149×25

c 234×32

d 194×37

e 245×14

f 376×12

g 246×28

h 319×45

i 462×38

Challenge

1

2	3	4	5	6

Use each of these digits once.

Arrange them to make a **product** as close as possible to

10 000

☐ ☐ ☐ × ☐ ☐

2

1	3	5	7	9

Use each of these digits once.

Arrange them to make a **product** as close as possible to

10 000

☐ ☐ ☐ × ☐ ☐

Short multiplication methods

Practice

1 Approximate the answer first.

2 Choose the standard method of recording you find the easiest to work out the answer to each calculation.

Example

$325 \times 42 \approx 300 \times 40 = 12\,000$

$$
\begin{array}{r}
325 \\
\times \quad 42 \\
\hline
\end{array}
$$

$(300 \times 42) \quad 12\,600$

$(20 \times 42) \quad\quad 840$

$(5 \times 42) \quad\quad 210$

$\quad\quad\quad\quad\quad 13\,650$

Remember

Remember to keep the numbers in the correct columns

Example

$325 \times 42 \approx 300 \times 40 = 12\,000$

$$
\begin{array}{r}
325 \\
\times \quad 42 \\
\hline
\end{array}
$$

$(325 \times 40) \quad 13\,000$

$(325 \times 2) \quad\quad 650$

$\quad\quad\quad\quad\quad 13\,650$

a 157 × 26

b 234 × 14

c 175 × 29

d 268 × 13

e 278 × 22

f 356 × 25

g 384 × 29

h 293 × 72

i 395 × 36

j 476 × 27

k 458 × 39

l 584 × 37

Refresher

Partition each of these calculations in 2 ways and work out the answers.

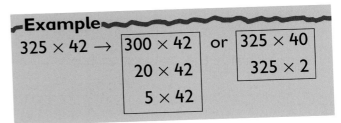

Example

$325 \times 42 \rightarrow$

300×42	or	325×40
20×42		325×2
5×42		

a 156×37

b 228×15

c 345×24

d 196×33

e 429×26

f 484×63

g 748×53

h 927×86

Challenge

Make up at least 3 word problems that involve calculations in the form of

☐ ☐ ☐ × ☐ ☐

using ideas from the picture.

Division methods

Practice

1 Approximate the answer to each calculation.

a	424 ÷ 18
b	636 ÷ 22
c	539 ÷ 11
d	672 ÷ 12

e	496 ÷ 25
f	764 ÷ 23
g	927 ÷ 32
h	878 ÷ 29

i	984 ÷ 24
j	793 ÷ 13
k	856 ÷ 27
l	395 ÷ 15

The "Guess the number of sweets" competition was won by 12 children. They had to share 624 sweets between them.

How many sweets did each child receive?

We can write this as a calculation:

624 ÷ 12 = ☐

We can work it out like this:

624 ÷ 12 ≈ 600 ÷ 12 = 50

```
 12 ) 624
  −  240   (20 × 12)
      384
  −  240   (20 × 12)
      144
  −  120   (10 × 12)
       24
  −   24    (2 × 12)
        0
```

Answer = 52

Each child gets 52 sweets.

2 Use the expanded method of division shown on the left to find the answers to each calculation.

a	455 ÷ 13	b	624 ÷ 16
c	946 ÷ 22	d	672 ÷ 24
e	480 ÷ 15	f	816 ÷ 12
g	806 ÷ 26	h	896 ÷ 32
i	459 ÷ 17	j	893 ÷ 19
k	966 ÷ 23	l	936 ÷ 18
m	546 ÷ 21	n	882 ÷ 14

3 The total cost of a 2-night camping holiday for 25 people is £575.

How much does each person pay?

4 There are 18 bookshelves and 774 books. Place the same number of books on each shelf. How many books are there on each shelf?

Refresher

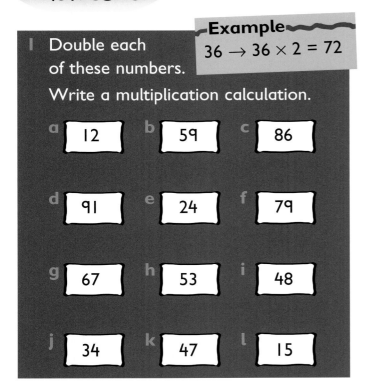

1 Double each of these numbers.

Example
36 → 36 × 2 = 72

Write a multiplication calculation.

a 12 b 59 c 86

d 91 e 24 f 79

g 67 h 53 i 48

j 34 k 47 l 15

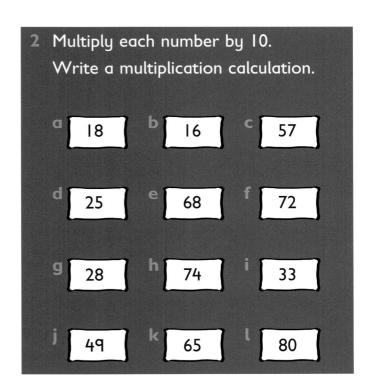

2 Multiply each number by 10.
Write a multiplication calculation.

a 18 b 16 c 57

d 25 e 68 f 72

g 28 h 74 i 33

j 49 k 65 l 80

Challenge

Write the calculations which have a remainder greater than $\frac{1}{2}$.

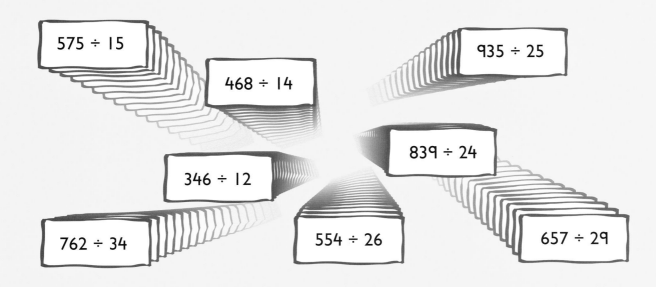

575 ÷ 15

468 ÷ 14

935 ÷ 25

839 ÷ 24

346 ÷ 12

762 ÷ 34

554 ÷ 26

657 ÷ 29

Long division

Practice

1 Approximate the answer first.

Use the standard method of recording to work out the answer to each calculation.

Try to work out the answer in as few steps as possible using multiples of 10 multiplied by the divisor.

a 754 ÷ 13 b 930 ÷ 15
c 912 ÷ 24 d 884 ÷ 26
e 882 ÷ 18 f 969 ÷ 17
g 957 ÷ 29 h 992 ÷ 32
i 952 ÷ 34 j 989 ÷ 43
k 864 ÷ 54 l 900 ÷ 25
m 768 ÷ 48 n 924 ÷ 33

A school's electricity bill for half the year is £832.

What is the cost per week?

We can write this as a calculation:

832 ÷ 26 = ☐

We can work it out like this:

832 ÷ 26 ≈ 900 ÷ 30 = 30

```
  26 ) 832
   −   780   (30 × 26)
        52
   −    52   (2 × 26)
         0
```

Answer = 32

The total cost per week is £32.

---

2 Find the answers to these word problems using the method above.

a A carton contains 672 pencils. Each box holds 12 pencils. How many boxes are there in the carton?

b The total bill for 24 nights' hotel accommodation is £936. How much does it cost per night?

c The Football Club has a lottery syndicate made up of 23 people. One week they win £966. How much does each person receive?

d A car uses 882l of petrol a fortnight. How many litres does it use on average per day?

Refresher

Work out the answers to these in your head.

1
a 150 ÷ 15
b 270 ÷ 27
c 320 ÷ 32
d 120 ÷ 12
e 240 ÷ 24
f 350 ÷ 35

2
a 300 ÷ 15
b 240 ÷ 12
c 360 ÷ 18
d 400 ÷ 20
e 280 ÷ 14
f 460 ÷ 23

3
a 450 ÷ 15
b 750 ÷ 25
c 480 ÷ 12
d 390 ÷ 13
e 440 ÷ 11
f 690 ÷ 23

4
a 770 ÷ 11
b 640 ÷ 32
c 600 ÷ 12
d 540 ÷ 60
e 450 ÷ 50

Challenge

Calculate the answers to these.

Reduce any remainder to its simplest form.

Example

$$595 ÷ 21 = 28 \text{ r } 7 = 28\frac{7}{21} = 28\frac{1}{3}$$

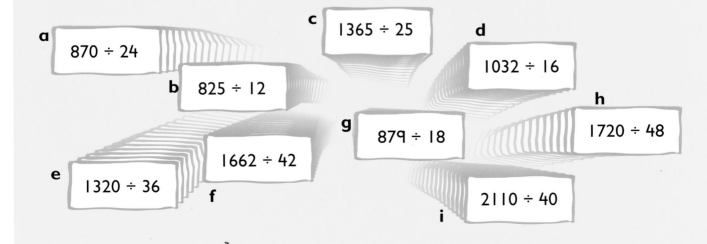

a 870 ÷ 24

b 825 ÷ 12

c 1365 ÷ 25

d 1032 ÷ 16

e 1320 ÷ 36

f 1662 ÷ 42

g 879 ÷ 18

h 1720 ÷ 48

i 2110 ÷ 40

Long division

Practice

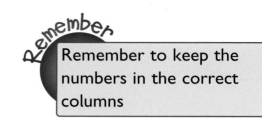

Remember to keep the numbers in the correct columns

1 Approximate the answer first.

Choose a standard method of recording to work out the answer to each calculation.

Example
555 ÷ 15 ≈ 600 ÷ 15 = 40

$$15 \overline{)555}$$
$$- \ 450 \quad (30 \times 15)$$
$$105$$
$$- \ 105 \quad (7 \times 15)$$
$$0$$

Answer = 37

or

Example
555 ÷ 15 ≈ 600 ÷ 15 = 40

$$15 \overline{)555} \quad 37$$
$$- \ 45$$
$$105$$
$$- \ 105$$
$$0$$

a 768 ÷ 16

b 621 ÷ 23

c 992 ÷ 32

d 931 ÷ 19

e 850 ÷ 25

f 984 ÷ 41

g 784 ÷ 14

h 816 ÷ 24

i 891 ÷ 27

j 972 ÷ 18

k 828 ÷ 36

l 841 ÷ 29

2 Use a calculator.

Use a multiplication calculation to check your answers.

Record what calculation you used to check each answer.

Example
555 ÷ 15 = ☐37☐ 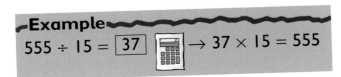 → 37 × 15 = 555

24

Refresher

Write the first 5 multiples of each of these numbers.

Example
$12 \rightarrow 12, 24, 36, 48, 60$

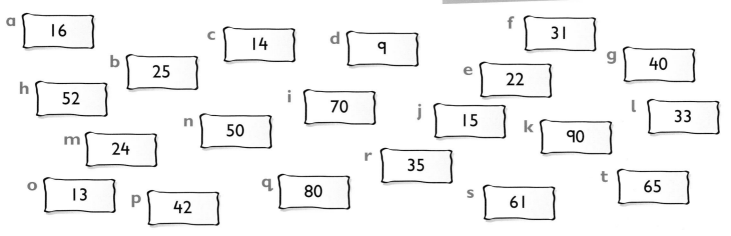

a 16

b 25

c 14

d 9

e 22

f 31

g 40

h 52

i 70

j 15

k 90

l 33

m 24

n 50

o 13

p 42

q 80

r 35

s 61

t 65

Challenge

1 Five answers total 49.
Can you find them?

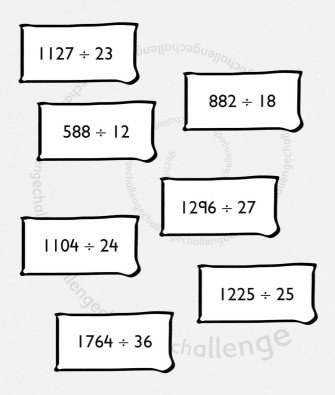

1127 ÷ 23

588 ÷ 12

882 ÷ 18

1296 ÷ 27

1104 ÷ 24

1225 ÷ 25

1764 ÷ 36

2 Which of these numbers are divisible by 16?

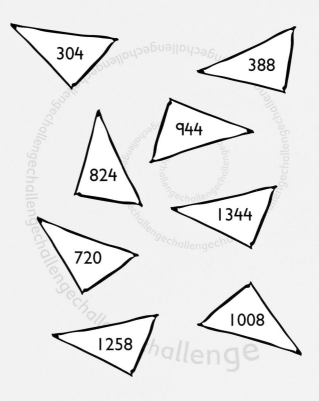

304

388

944

824

1344

720

1258

1008

25

Solving word problems

Practice

James went through the classified ads in the newspaper. He circled the ones he was interested in. Answer the questions below about each ad.

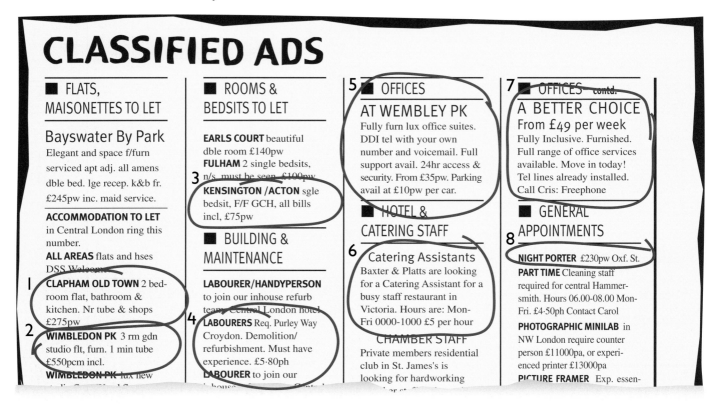

1 James wants to rent for 6 months. How much will he pay?

2 What is the cost per year? Bills make up 10% of the monthly rent. How much will he pay for bills?

3 How much will James spend on rent in 1 year?

4 How much does a labourer earn for working 8 hours?
How much for a 40-hour week?

5 How much do these offices cost to rent per year?
What is the total cost if you rent an office and park 2 cars for 1 year?

6 How much do you earn for working a 39-hour week?
25% is deducted from your wage for tax. How much money do you take home?

7 How much do you pay for office space for 1 year?

8 A night porter works 5 nights per week. How much does he earn per night?

Refresher

1 Find the answers to these. Show any remainders as fractions.

   a $66 \div 8$
   b $75 \div 9$
   c $124 \div 6$
   d $95 \div 9$
   e $181 \div 3$
   f $216 \div 7$
   g $242 \div 8$
   h $105 \div 10$
   i $56 \div 6$
   j $83 \div 4$
   k $252 \div 10$
   l $162 \div 4$
   m $93 \div 5$
   n $366 \div 9$

2 Divide these amounts in pounds by the number given. Give your answer in £.p.

   a £1 ÷ 4
   b £5 ÷ 10
   c £3 ÷ 3
   d £8 ÷ 5
   e £60 ÷ 12
   f £80 ÷ 20
   g £9 ÷ 5
   h £2 ÷ 5
   i £5 ÷ 4
   j £4 ÷ 5
   k £7 ÷ 2
   l £55 ÷ 11
   m £101 ÷ 20
   n £10 ÷ 4

Challenge

James has a choice of properties to rent.

a

One double bedroom Victorian conversion flat · small study/storage room · fitted kitchen · bathroom · patio garden · furnished · available now

£205 per week

b

Two double bedroom house · reception room · fitted kitchen · bathroom · separate WC · patio garden · superb location · moments from the Wandsworth Town mainline · available furnished

£315 per week

c

A well presented three/four bedroom ground floor period maisonette · ideal central location · stylish neutral decor · spacious reception · available now

£324 per week

1 Work out how much each property will cost over the year.

2 Work out how much each property will cost to rent per month.

3 James has a maximum of £1375 to spend on rent per month. Which property should he choose, a, b, or c?

Computer word problems

Practice

Read the word problems.

Choose an appropriate method of calculating your answer.

- mental
- mental with jottings
- paper and pencil (standard method)
- calculator

a Work out the total cost of each item including VAT at 17·5%.

b Buy the computer and the printer as a package and get 20% off the total price. How much do you pay including VAT?

c Buy 1 of each item. What is the total cost before VAT? What is the cost after VAT is added?

d The shop is offering a 25% discount if you buy 2 mobile phones. What is the total cost including VAT?

e The shop is offering £5 of free calls with every mobile phone sold. Calls cost 10p per minute peak time and 5p per minute off-peak. How many minutes can you speak for free in peak and off-peak times?

f In the sale, the lap-top will be reduced in price by 10% before VAT. What will be the new price? How much will you pay, including VAT?

£850

£260

£1020

£380

£40

Prices are exclusive of VAT at 17·5%

Refresher

Use the items and prices from the Practice activity to work out the answers to these questions. You will not need to include VAT on any of the items.

a The shop sells 7 computers in one day. How much money do they make?

b 2 lap-tops are sold each day Monday to Saturday. How much money does the shop make?

c The shop has 56 digital cameras in stock. What is their total value?

d The shop has 100 lap-tops to sell. How much money will they make?

e The shop is planning a sale. All items above £500 will be reduced by 20%. What is the new price of each item?

f In the sale, all items below £500 will be reduced by 15%. What is the new price of each item?

Challenge

Use the prices and the items in the Practice activity to work out the answers.

A local business buys 2 of each of the items.

1 Calculate the total cost including VAT at 17·5%.

2 They spread the payments over a 12-month period at an extra cost of 25% interest. What is the new total cost? What is the monthly payment?

Ordering fractions

Practice

1 Order these fractions. First convert them to equivalent fractions, then draw a number line and write the fractions.

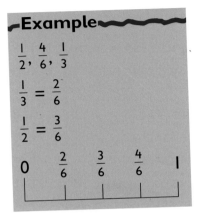

Example

$\frac{1}{2}$, $\frac{4}{6}$, $\frac{1}{3}$

$\frac{1}{3} = \frac{2}{6}$

$\frac{1}{2} = \frac{3}{6}$

0    $\frac{2}{6}$ $\frac{3}{6}$ $\frac{4}{6}$ 1

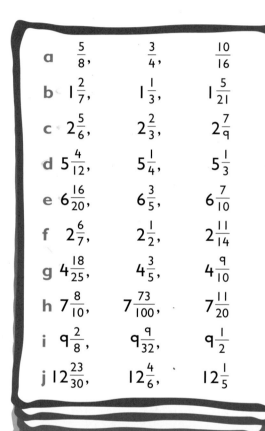

a $\frac{5}{8}$, $\frac{3}{4}$, $\frac{10}{16}$

b $1\frac{2}{7}$, $1\frac{1}{3}$, $1\frac{5}{21}$

c $2\frac{5}{6}$, $2\frac{2}{3}$, $2\frac{7}{9}$

d $5\frac{4}{12}$, $5\frac{1}{4}$, $5\frac{1}{3}$

e $6\frac{16}{20}$, $6\frac{3}{5}$, $6\frac{7}{10}$

f $2\frac{6}{7}$, $2\frac{1}{2}$, $2\frac{11}{14}$

g $4\frac{18}{25}$, $4\frac{3}{5}$, $4\frac{9}{10}$

h $7\frac{8}{10}$, $7\frac{73}{100}$, $7\frac{11}{20}$

i $9\frac{2}{8}$, $9\frac{9}{32}$, $9\frac{1}{2}$

j $12\frac{23}{30}$, $12\frac{4}{6}$, $12\frac{1}{5}$

2 What number is halfway between these numbers?

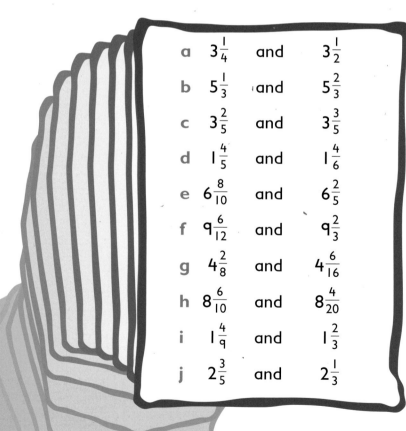

a $3\frac{1}{4}$ and $3\frac{1}{2}$

b $5\frac{1}{3}$ and $5\frac{2}{3}$

c $3\frac{2}{5}$ and $3\frac{3}{5}$

d $1\frac{4}{5}$ and $1\frac{4}{6}$

e $6\frac{8}{10}$ and $6\frac{2}{5}$

f $9\frac{6}{12}$ and $9\frac{2}{3}$

g $4\frac{2}{8}$ and $4\frac{6}{16}$

h $8\frac{6}{10}$ and $8\frac{4}{20}$

i $1\frac{4}{9}$ and $1\frac{2}{3}$

j $2\frac{3}{5}$ and $2\frac{1}{3}$

Refresher

Order these fractions by first converting them to equivalent fractions.

a	$\frac{1}{2}$	$\frac{3}{8}$	$\frac{1}{4}$
b	$\frac{3}{4}$	$\frac{7}{8}$	$\frac{2}{3}$
c	$\frac{1}{3}$	$\frac{4}{6}$	$\frac{1}{2}$
d	$\frac{1}{4}$	$\frac{5}{8}$	$\frac{1}{2}$
e	$\frac{2}{5}$	$\frac{3}{4}$	$\frac{6}{10}$
f	$\frac{7}{12}$	$\frac{1}{4}$	$\frac{2}{3}$
g	$\frac{7}{10}$	$\frac{12}{20}$	$\frac{4}{5}$
h	$\frac{4}{6}$	$\frac{9}{12}$	$\frac{1}{3}$
i	$\frac{7}{9}$	$\frac{2}{3}$	$\frac{14}{18}$
j	$\frac{9}{12}$	$\frac{1}{2}$	$\frac{5}{6}$
k	$\frac{11}{15}$	$\frac{1}{5}$	$\frac{2}{3}$
l	$\frac{3}{5}$	$\frac{7}{30}$	$\frac{2}{6}$

Convert these fractions to eighths.

Convert these fractions to twenty-fourths.

Convert these fractions to sixths.

Convert these fractions to eighths.

Convert these fractions to twentieths.

Challenge

Work in pairs. Draw one number line on a piece of paper. Each person writes a fraction. Convert both fractions to a fraction with a common denominator. Put them on the number line.

Repeat four more times.

Remember

Think carefully where the fractions go on the number line!

31

What's my partner?

Practice

1 Work out the decimal equivalent for these fractions.
Use a calculator. Show your working.

You will need to round some decimals to 3 places.

a $\frac{3}{8}$ b $\frac{5}{9}$ c $\frac{6}{13}$

d $\frac{16}{20}$ e $\frac{1}{6}$ f $\frac{19}{25}$

g $\frac{2}{3}$ h $\frac{5}{6}$ i $\frac{3}{20}$

j $\frac{7}{15}$ k $\frac{3}{16}$ l $\frac{5}{14}$

2 Work out the **simplest** fraction equivalent for these decimals. Show your working.

a 0·76 b 0·586 c 0·06

d 0·92 e 0·265 f 0·108

g 0·94 h 0·12 i 0·689

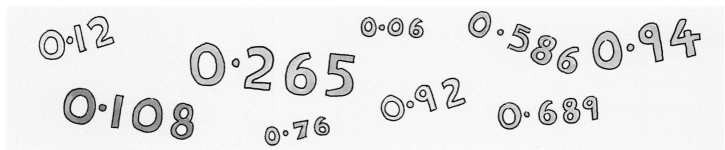

Refresher

1 What is the decimal equivalent for these fractions? Try and remember these "pairs".

a $\frac{1}{2}$ b $\frac{1}{4}$ c $\frac{3}{4}$ d $\frac{1}{5}$ e $\frac{1}{10}$

2 Work out the decimal equivalent for these fractions using a calculator.

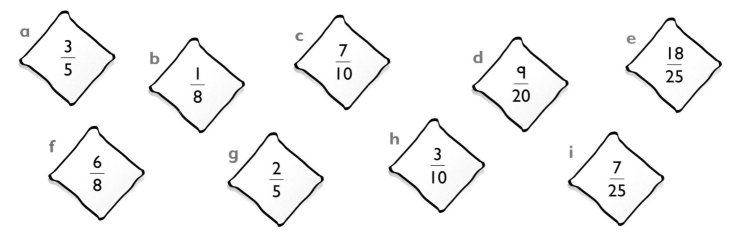

a $\frac{3}{5}$ b $\frac{1}{8}$ c $\frac{7}{10}$ d $\frac{9}{20}$ e $\frac{18}{25}$

f $\frac{6}{8}$ g $\frac{2}{5}$ h $\frac{3}{10}$ i $\frac{7}{25}$

Challenge

Work out the fraction and decimal equivalent for these percentages. Make sure the fraction is in its simplest form.

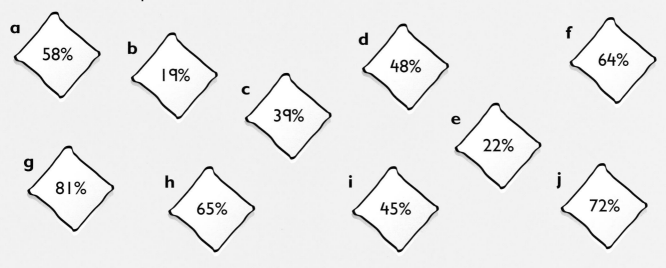

a 58%   b 19%   c 39%   d 48%   e 22%   f 64%

g 81%   h 65%   i 45%   j 72%

Convert and compare

Practice

Order the fractions by converting them to decimals.

Use a calculator. You will need to round some decimals to 3 places.

a $\frac{4}{7}$ $\frac{3}{11}$ $\frac{2}{5}$

b $\frac{7}{12}$ $\frac{6}{15}$ $\frac{4}{9}$

c $\frac{13}{18}$ $\frac{8}{12}$ $\frac{4}{5}$

d $\frac{7}{20}$ $\frac{1}{7}$ $\frac{5}{13}$

e $\frac{6}{11}$ $\frac{9}{17}$ $\frac{3}{8}$

f $\frac{18}{21}$ $\frac{7}{13}$ $\frac{4}{10}$

g $\frac{63}{100}$ $\frac{4}{9}$ $\frac{6}{15}$

h $\frac{8}{10}$ $\frac{784}{1000}$ $\frac{96}{100}$

i $\frac{4}{14}$ $\frac{9}{24}$ $\frac{13}{34}$

j $\frac{1}{2}$ $\frac{5}{8}$ $\frac{67}{100}$

k $\frac{9}{17}$ $\frac{13}{24}$ $\frac{6}{9}$

l $\frac{4}{7}$ $\frac{3}{8}$ $\frac{2}{9}$

m $\frac{4}{16}$ $\frac{2}{11}$ $\frac{5}{21}$

n $\frac{12}{100}$ $\frac{1}{8}$ $\frac{1}{9}$

o $\frac{7}{23}$ $\frac{5}{6}$ $\frac{561}{1000}$

p $\frac{3}{4}$ $\frac{6}{7}$ $\frac{11}{13}$

q $\frac{1}{9}$ $\frac{3}{17}$ $\frac{4}{22}$

r $\frac{28}{100}$ $\frac{8}{12}$ $\frac{9}{13}$

s $\frac{5}{7}$ $\frac{7}{8}$ $\frac{83}{1000}$

t $\frac{9}{26}$ $\frac{3}{11}$ $\frac{33}{100}$

u $\frac{4}{5}$ $\frac{12}{14}$ $\frac{19}{23}$

Refresher

Order the fractions by converting them to decimals. Use a calculator.

a $\frac{4}{5}$ $\frac{2}{3}$

b $\frac{3}{8}$ $\frac{5}{20}$

c $\frac{96}{100}$ $\frac{9}{10}$

d $\frac{21}{25}$ $\frac{5}{8}$

e $\frac{1}{6}$ $\frac{2}{8}$

f $\frac{1}{3}$ $\frac{7}{20}$

g $\frac{68}{100}$ $\frac{3}{5}$

h $\frac{3}{4}$ $\frac{16}{20}$

i $\frac{3}{25}$ $\frac{1}{10}$

j $\frac{7}{8}$ $\frac{8}{10}$

k $\frac{2}{5}$ $\frac{8}{25}$

l $\frac{37}{100}$ $\frac{3}{10}$

Challenge

Copy these pyramids. Convert the fractions to decimals so that you can add them and complete the pyramid. Add the two bricks together and write the total in the brick above.

a

$4\frac{3}{5}$ $2\frac{4}{7}$ $1\frac{9}{15}$ $5\frac{2}{9}$

b

6·91

$\frac{6}{8}$ $6\frac{2}{12}$ $5\frac{7}{17}$ $2\frac{9}{14}$

Decimal order

Practice

1 Order the decimals from smallest to largest.

a	3·2	3·26	3·02	3·254	3·367	3·102
b	5·95	5·903	5·9	5·921	5·2	5·59
c	7·426	7·406	7·4	7·41	7·004	7·04
d	8·183	8·1	8·83	8·103	8·11	8·8
e	1·7	1·75	1·755	1·577	1·57	1·55
f	2·88	2·841	2·14	2·8	2·889	2·1
g	9·006	9·06	9·66	9·69	9·669	9·6
h	0·4	0·456	0·56	0·402	0·004	0·04
i	0·22	0·225	0·2	0·26	0·226	0·62
j	1·8	1·88	1·888	1·808	1·899	1·98

2 What decimals come between these numbers?

a	12·6	and	12·61	b	30·54	and	30·548
c	24·6	and	24·609	d	72·99	and	73·001
e	15·47	and	15·479	f	62·01	and	62·1
g	54·81	and	54·817	h	38·421	and	38·43
i	14·991	and	15·005	j	29·04	and	29·17

Refresher

Order the decimals from smallest to largest.

a	3·4	3·45	3·5	3·54	3·55	3·44
b	7·2	7·26	7·27	7·19	7·3	7·62
c	9·11	9·19	9·1	9·2	9·28	9·18
d	4·68	4·86	4·9	4·8	4·18	4·92
e	1·71	1·07	1·7	1·17	1·77	1·75
f	2·5	2·58	2·73	2·8	2·49	2·1
g	5·8	5·64	5·18	5·1	5·46	5·49
h	12·9	12·84	12·62	12·8	12·2	12·48
i	24·7	24·5	24·75	24·93	24·17	24·9
j	48·05	48·5	48·55	48·25	48·2	48·3
k	33·82	33·28	33·8	33·03	33·3	33·6
l	18·9	18·29	18·09	18·2	18·92	18·02
m	71·6	71·86	71·8	71·48	71·4	71·06
n	48·29	48·73	48·6	48·1	48·99	48·72
o	36·03	36·82	36·1	36·9	36·72	36·3

Challenge

Copy out the numbers and arrows. Label each arrow with the difference between the numbers.

Example

0·83

a 3·27 ⌒ 4·1

a 3·27   4·1   5·695   6·7   7·01   8

b 1·5   1·963   2·37   4·4   5·18   6

c 2·102   2·9   3·54   4·77   5·6   7

d 5·88   6·1   7·482   8·3   8·66   9

e 4·2   4·596   5·3   6·48   7·03   8

Decimal battleships

Practice

A game for 2 players

● Both players copy the grid below.

● Write a number between 5 and 10 with two decimal places in each space, for example, 6·49. Don't let your partner see your numbers.

● Choose 4 of your numbers and put a circle around them. These are your bonus numbers.

● Take it in turns to call out a number with **one** decimal place, for example 9·3. If the number your partner calls out is the closest tenth to one of your numbers, then you must put a line through that number. You can only cross out one number each time.

● Write down all the numbers you call out. Stop when you have both called out 20 numbers.

● Count how many of your numbers have not been crossed out. Any bonus numbers not crossed out are counted as two.

● The player with the highest score is the winner.

Refresher

1 Round these numbers to the nearest whole number.

a 7·23   b 6·39

c 4·12   d 9·02

e 7·85   f 6·84

g 3·22   h 7·49

i 8·61   j 5·01

2 Round these numbers to the nearest tenth.

a 2·38   b 1·09

c 5·69   d 2·51

e 7·49   f 6·33

g 4·91   h 1·99

i 3·82   j 7·61

Decimal battleships

Play the game in the Practice section with these changes:

● Write numbers with one decimal place between 0 and 10 in the grid, for example, 5·8.

● Call out whole numbers between 0 and 10. If the number your partner calls out is the closest whole number to one of your numbers, put a line through that number. You can only cross out one number each time.

Challenge

Round these numbers to the nearest tenth.

Example
6·314 → 6·3

a 7·235   b 6·342   c 7·465   d 3·001   e 4·025

f 8·409   g 6·738   h 2·951   i 9·834   j 1·499

Triangle fractions, decimals and percentages

Practice

1 Copy and complete the following triangles.

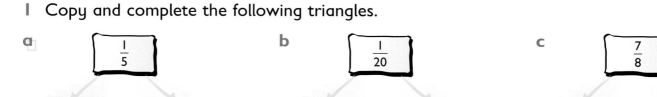

a
$\frac{1}{5}$

20%

·

b
$\frac{1}{20}$

%

·

c
$\frac{7}{8}$

%

·

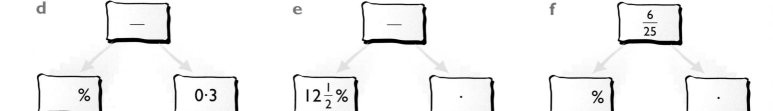

d
—

%

0·3

e
—

$12\frac{1}{2}$%

·

f
$\frac{6}{25}$

%

·

g
—

%

0·35

h
$\frac{2}{3}$

%

·

i
—

%

0·78

j
$\frac{5}{8}$

%

·

k
—

96%

·

l
—

%

0·9

2 Now make up some of your own.

Refresher

Copy and complete the table. Use a calculator to work out the missing decimals and percentages.

Fraction		Decimal	Percentage
a	$\frac{1}{2}$	$1 \div 2 = 0\cdot\boxed{}$	$100 \div 2 = \boxed{}\ \%$
b	$\frac{1}{4}$	$1 \div 4 = 0\cdot\boxed{}$	$100 \div 4 = \boxed{}\ \%$
c	$\frac{1}{5}$	$1 \div 5 = 0\cdot\boxed{}$	$100 \div 5 = \boxed{}\ \%$
d	$\frac{1}{3}$	$1 \div 3 = 0\cdot\boxed{}$	$100 \div 3 = \boxed{}\ \%$
e	$\frac{1}{8}$	$1 \div 8 = 0\cdot\boxed{}$	$100 \div 8 = \boxed{}\ \%$
f	$\frac{1}{10}$	$1 \div 10 = 0\cdot\boxed{}$	$100 \div 10 = \boxed{}\ \%$
g	$\frac{3}{4}$	$1 \div 4 = 0\cdot\boxed{} \quad 0\cdot\boxed{} \times 3 = 0\cdot\boxed{}$	$100 \div 4 = \boxed{}\ \% \quad \boxed{}\ \% \times 3 = \boxed{}\ \%$

Challenge
Fraction dice

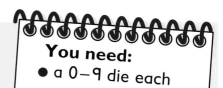

You need:
- a 0–9 die each

For two players

- Both throw your die and make a fraction. It must not be a top heavy fraction, for example, 7 and 3 becomes $\frac{3}{7}$.
- Convert your fraction to a decimal. Compare your decimal to your partner's. The highest decimal gets a point.
- Keep going until one player gets 10 points.

Percentage squares

Practice

Work out the percentages in the corners of the amount of the number in the middle.
Record your calculations.

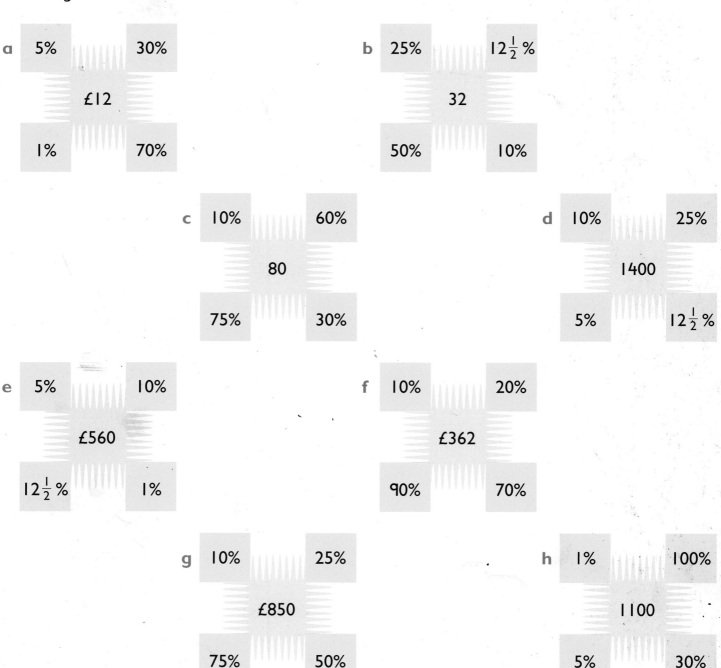

a
5%   30%
£12
1%   70%

b
25% $12\frac{1}{2}$ %
32
50%   10%

c
10%   60%
80
75%   30%

d
10%   25%
1400
5% $12\frac{1}{2}$ %

e
5%   10%
£560
$12\frac{1}{2}$ %   1%

f
10%   20%
£362
90%   70%

g
10%   25%
£850
75%   50%

h
1%   100%
1100
5%   30%

Refresher

Example

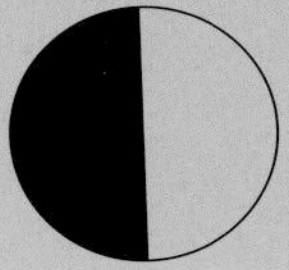

50%

What percentage of each shape is shaded?

a

b

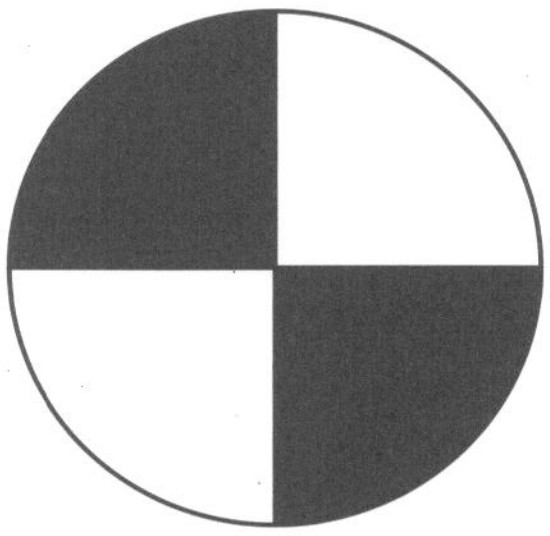

c

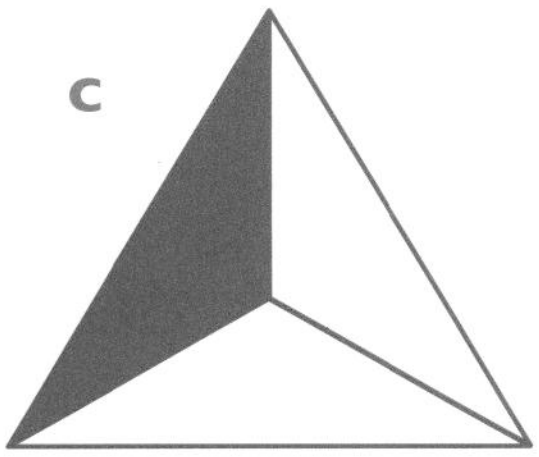

d

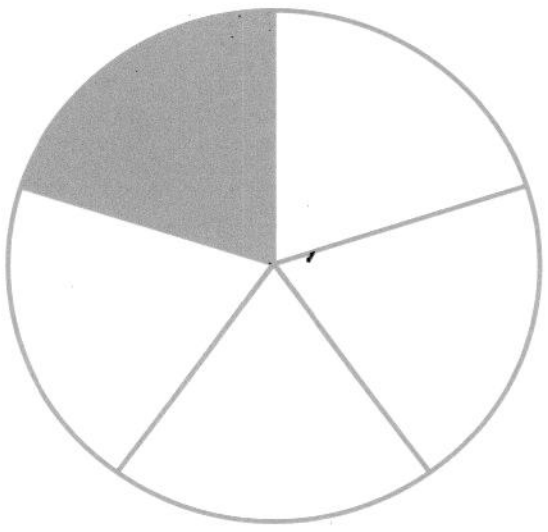

e

f

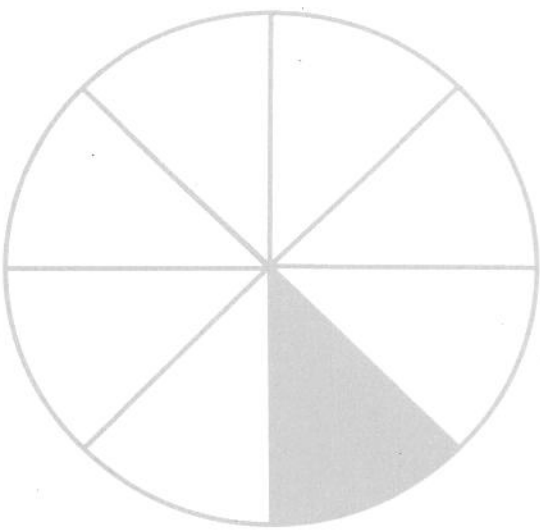

g

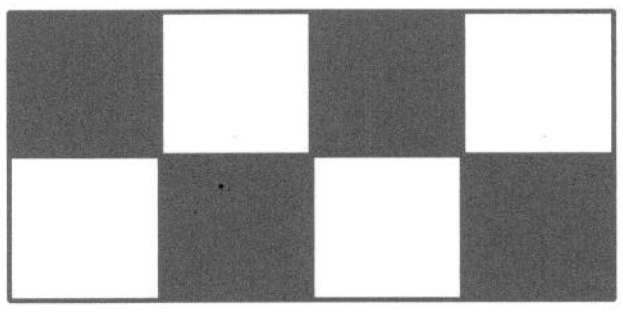

h

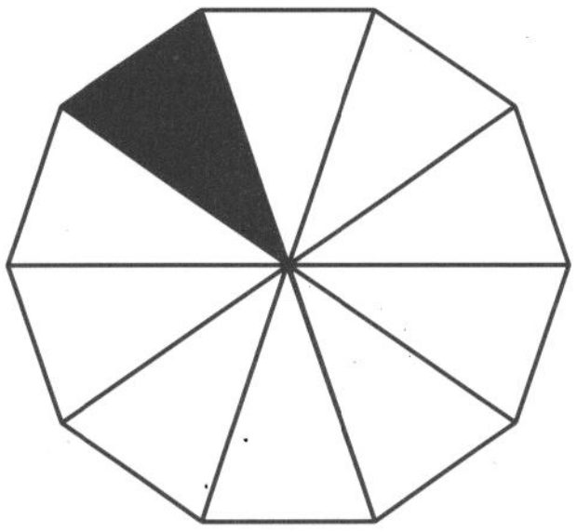

i

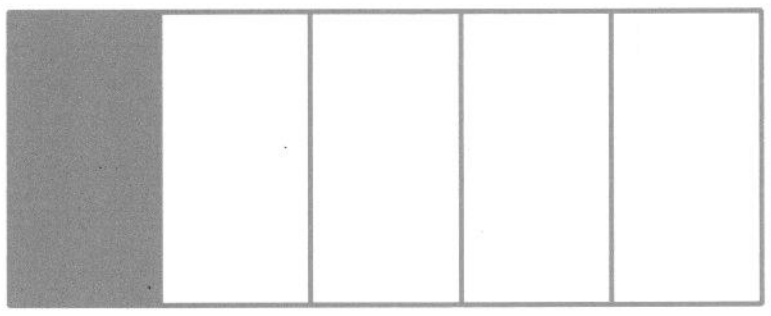

j

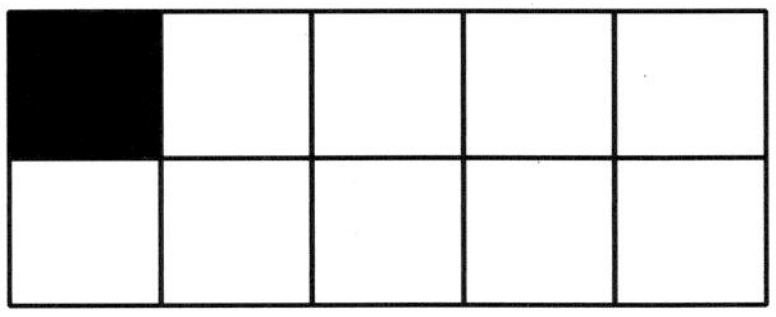

k

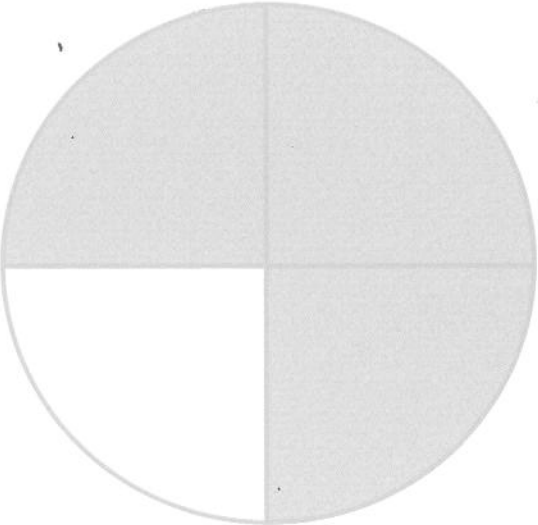

Challenge

Example

4 is 50% of 8

1   Complete this statement in as many ways as you can.

4 is ☐ % of ☐

2   Now repeat for these statements:

15 is ☐ % of ☐   3·20 is ☐ % of ☐   4·32 is ☐ % of ☐

Shop percentages

Practice

1 The clothing shop is going to close down in 5 days. Over the next week everything must be sold.

On Monday the prices will be reduced by 10%.

On Tuesday the prices will be reduced by 15%.

On Wednesday the prices will be reduced by 30%.

On Thursday the prices will be reduced by 50%.

On Friday the prices will be reduced by 75%.

Work out the prices of the following items for each day over the next week.

a £15 – T-shirt

b £27·60 – Shirt

c £45 – Jacket

d £32 – Dress

e £51 – Trousers

f £63·40 – Suit

2 At the supermarket you get extra free. Work out what percentage is free.

a 440 g for the price of 400 g

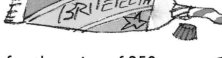

b 300 g for the price of 250 g

c 100 g for the price of 75 g

d 9 l for the price of 8 l

e 21 biscuits for the price of 20

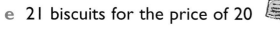

Refresher

The stationery shop is going to close down in 5 days.
Over the next week everything must be sold.
On Monday the prices will be reduced by 10%.
On Tuesday the prices will be reduced by 20%.
On Wednesday the prices will be reduced by 30%.
On Thursday the prices will be reduced by 50%.
On Friday the prices will be reduced by 75%.
Work out the prices of the following items
over the next week.

£5·20

£2

£3·80

£1·80

£2·60

£4

Example

Pencils

£1·60

Monday	£1·44
Tuesday	£1·28
Wednesday	£1·12
Thursday	80p
Friday	40p

Challenge

You own a shop. You are going to have a sale. Work out the original prices for 10 items
and the percentage you are going to reduce them by.
Ask a friend to calculate your sale prices.

Ratio and proportion with shapes

Practice

Describe the relationship between the two shapes using ratio and proportion.

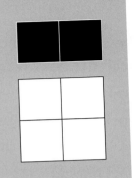

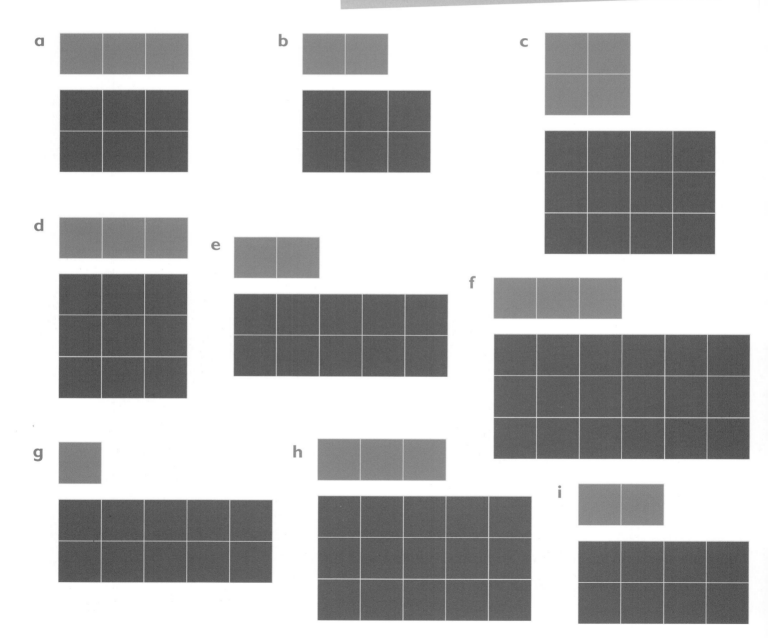

Refresher

Write the ratio and proportion of the patterns.

Example

The ratio of black squares to white squares is 1 to every 5.

The proportion of black squares to white squares is 1 in every 6.

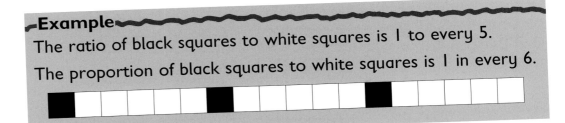

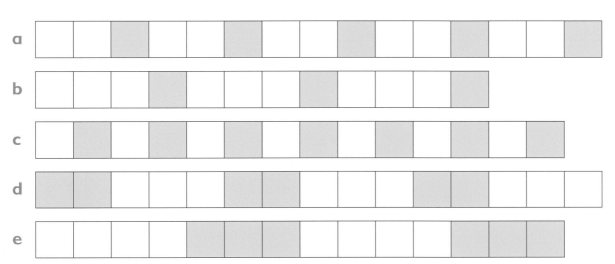

a

b

c

d

e

Challenge

What is the ratio of the distance around your head to your height?

Is the ratio the same for other people?

Do adults have the same ratio?

Ratio and proportion

Practice

1 For every 2 pages of a book that Jill reads, Jack reads 6.

  a What is the ratio of pages read by Jill to the pages read by Jack?

  b What is the proportion of pages read by Jill?

  c What is the proportion of pages read by Jack?

  d If Jack reads 36 pages how many will Jill have read?

  e If Jill reads 8 pages how many will Jack have read?

2 Anne and Tony have made 28 cakes. Anne ate 8 of the cakes and Tony ate the rest.

  a What is the ratio of cakes eaten by Anne to cakes eaten by Tony?

  b What is the proportion of cakes eaten by Anne?

  c What is the proportion of cakes eaten by Tony?

  d When Anne had eaten 4 of the cakes how many had Tony eaten?

  e When Tony had eaten 15 of the cakes how many had Anne eaten?

3 In a box of chocolates, there are 3 plain chocolates to every 5 milk chocolates.

  a What is the ratio of plain chocolates to milk chocolates?

  b What is the proportion of plain chocolates?

  c What is the proportion of milk chocolates?

  d If there are 15 plain chocolates, what will be the total number of chocolates?

  e If there are 40 milk chocolates, what will be the total number of chocolates?

4 The recipe says that to make a sauce, you need $1\frac{1}{2}$ litres of water to every $\frac{1}{2}$ litre of milk.

  a What is the ratio of water to milk?

  b What is the proportion of water?

  c What is the proportion of milk?

  d If 10 litres of sauce are made, how much milk will be used?

  e If 4 litres of milk are used, how much sauce will be made?

Refresher

1   I can swim 40 m for every 10 m my friend swims.

  a   If I swim 160 m, how far will my friend swim?

  b   If my friend swims 60 m, how far will I swim?

  c   If we swim 300 m in total, how far will each of us have swum?

2   For every 2 days it rained last month, it was sunny for 3.

  a   If it rained for 8 days, how many days was it sunny?

  b   If it was sunny for 15 days, how many days did it rain?

  c   Over 30 days, how many sunny days and how many rainy days were there?

3   For every 60p pocket money I get, I save 20p and spend 40p.

  a   If I save 80p how much do I spend?

  b   If I spend £2 how much do I save?

  c   If I am given £6 pocket money, how much do I spend and how much do I save?

Challenge

1   I made 30 cakes and ate $\frac{1}{5}$ of them. My sister ate the rest.

  a   What proportion of the cakes did I eat?

  b   What proportion of the cakes did my sister eat?

  c   What is the ratio of cakes eaten by me to cakes eaten by my sister?

2   I saved 40% of my money. I have £12 saved.

  a   What proportion of the money did I spend?

  b   What proportion of the money did I save?

  c   What is the ratio of money saved to money spent?

3   I had 24 sweets. I gave my brother $\frac{1}{3}$ of them.

  a   What proportion of the sweets did I have?

  b   What proportion of the sweets did my brother have?

  c   What is the ratio of my sweets to my brother's sweets?

Fractions and frequencies

Practice

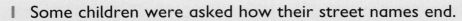

Cancel all fractions to their lowest terms.

1 Some children were asked how their street names end.

a What is the total frequency?

b What fraction of street names end in Avenue?

c What fraction of street names end in Street?

d What fraction of street names end in Close?

e What fraction of street names end in Close or Road?

Street name	Number
Street	6
Avenue	8
Close	3
Road	9
Total	

2 The table shows the number of children in some families.

a What is the total frequency?

b What fraction of families have 1 child?

c What fraction of families have 3 children?

d What fraction of families have 2 children?

e What fraction of families have 4 children?

Children	Families
1	10
2	5
3	15
4	11
5	4
Total	

3 The table shows the number of pets in children's homes.

a Use the following information to complete the table.

$\frac{1}{4}$ of homes have no pets.

$\frac{1}{3}$ of homes have 1 pet.

$\frac{1}{6}$ of homes have 3 pets.

b What fraction of homes have 2 pets?

Pets	Homes
0	
1	
2	
3	
Total	36

4 The table shows the number of bedrooms in a street of houses.

a Use the following information to complete the table.

$\frac{1}{10}$ of the houses have 1 bedroom.

$\frac{2}{5}$ of the houses have 2 bedrooms.

$\frac{3}{10}$ of the houses have 4 bedrooms.

b What fraction of houses have 3 bedrooms?

Bedrooms	Houses
1	
2	
3	
4	
Total	40

Refresher

1 Some children were asked the colour of their front door.

   a What fraction of the doors are red?

   b What fraction of the doors are blue?

   c What fraction of the doors are red or blue?

   d What fraction of the doors are brown or red?

   e What fraction of the doors are not red?

Colour	Number
Red	2
Blue	5
White	1
Brown	2
Total	**10**

2 Some children were asked how many brothers they have.

   a What fraction of children have 1 brother?

   b What fraction of children have no brothers?

   c What fraction of children have 1 or 2 brothers?

   d What fraction of children have 2 or 3 brothers?

   e What fraction of children have at least 1 brother?

Brothers	Number
0	4
1	3
2	3
3	2
Total	**12**

Challenge

The tables show the number of bedrooms in the houses of two streets.

1 a Which street has the greatest fraction of 1 bedroom houses?

   b Which street has the greatest fraction of 2 bedroom houses?

   c Which street has the greatest fraction of 3 bedroom houses?

   d Which street has the greatest fraction of 4 bedroom houses?

2 a What fraction of houses in Greenfield Close have 1 or 2 bedrooms?

   b Compare this with Maybury Road.

Greenfield Close

Bedrooms	Houses
1	1
2	3
3	4
4	2
Total	

Maybury Road

Bedrooms	Houses
1	5
2	8
3	4
4	3
Total	

Percentages and frequencies

Practice

Work in pairs.

You need:
- one calculator each
- a 1–6 die each

1   Both copy this tally chart.

2   One person rolls a die 10 times.
    The other rolls a die 20 times.
    Record your results in your tally chart.

3   Convert the frequencies to fractions.
    Write them on the chart.

4   Convert the fractions to percentages.
    Write them on the chart.

5   Which person rolled the greatest
    percentage of these numbers?
    Write down your own percentage.

Die number	Tally	Frequency	Fraction	%
1				
2				
3				
4				
5				
6				
Total				

    a 2   b 5   c even

    d above 2   e 1 or 6   f below 4

6   Make new tally charts.

7   This time, one person rolls a die 24 times, the other person, 32 times.

8   Convert the frequencies to fractions. Write them on the chart.

9   Convert the fractions to percentages. Use your calculator.
    Round your answers to the nearest whole percentage. Write them on the chart.

10 Which person rolled the greatest percentage of these numbers?

    a 1   b 3   c odd

    d 2 or 5   e less than 3   f more than 1

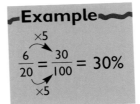

Example

$$\overset{\times 5}{\frac{6}{20}} = \frac{30}{100} = 30\%$$
$$\underset{\times 5}{}$$

Refresher

1 Convert these fractions to percentages.

a $\frac{9}{20}$ b $\frac{7}{10}$ c $\frac{17}{20}$ d $\frac{3}{10}$ e $\frac{12}{20}$

f $\frac{20}{50}$ g $\frac{4}{25}$ h $\frac{9}{10}$ i $\frac{26}{50}$ j $\frac{21}{25}$

2 Convert these fractions to percentages.
Use your calculator. Round your answers
to the nearest whole percentage.

Example

$\frac{13}{24} = 54\%$

(calculate $13 \div 24 \times 100$)

a $\frac{7}{24}$ b $\frac{15}{32}$ c $\frac{19}{24}$ d $\frac{25}{32}$ e $\frac{3}{32}$

f $\frac{9}{40}$ g $\frac{27}{38}$ h $\frac{425}{700}$ i $\frac{93}{120}$ j $\frac{71}{230}$

Challenge

1 40 residents in Huddlestone Road
voted in a local election.

The table shows the percentage of
votes for each party.

a Copy the table.

b Calculate the votes for each party.

Party	Votes	Percentage
Labour		25%
Conservative		20%
Liberal Democrat		45%
Others		10%
Total	40	

2 60 residents of Stumblemead Road
voted in the same local election.

The table shows the percentage of
votes for each party.

a Copy the table.

b Calculate the votes for each party.

Party	Votes	Percentage
Labour		40%
Conservative		15%
Liberal Democrat		
Others		10%
Total		

Spending pie charts

You need:
● a calculator

Practice

1 The pie charts show how Maria and Jamaine spent their birthday money.

a Find the fraction they spent on each item.

b Calculate the amount they spent on each item.

c Copy and complete the tables.

Maria
- books ■ clothes
- handbags

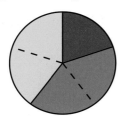

Total spent = £30

Item	Fraction	Money spent (£)
books		
handbags		
clothes		
Total		

Jamaine
- computer game ■ clothes
- bicycle wheel □ magazines

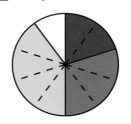

Total spent = £65

Item	Fraction	Money spent (£)
Total		

2 The pie charts show how two families spent their holiday money.

Make a table for each family.

Wilkins family
- ■ guest house
- ■ entertainment
- □ eating out ■ car hire

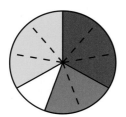

Total spent = £819

Baxter family
- ■ caravan sites
- ■ entertainment
- ■ fuel □ food etc.

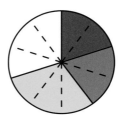

Total spent = £740

Refresher

The pie charts show how Jane and Ken spent their book vouchers.

Find the fraction they spent on each book.

Calculate the amount they spent on each book.

Copy and complete the tables.

Book	Money spent (£)
space	
horses	
puzzles	
magazines	
Total	

Book	Money spent (£)
adventure	
computers	
history	
Total	

Jane's books
- ■ space ■ horses
- puzzles □ magazines

Ken's books
- ■ adventure ■ computers
- history

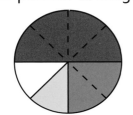

Total spent = £24

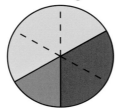

Total spent = £18

Challenge

You need:
- a pair of compasses

1 The table shows how Solomon spent his pocket money.

  a Calculate the fraction he spent on each item.

  b Sketch a pie chart for the table. Colour the sectors and make a key.

Item	Money spent (£)	Fraction
Geometry set	2	
Sweets	1	
Cinema	3	
Magazine	2	
Total		

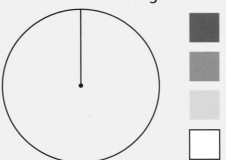

2 Draw pie charts for these tables.

Item	Money spent (£)
Calculator	8
Pencil set	4
Music CD	12
Total	

Item	Money spent (£)
Shoes	21
Dress	14
Trousers	21
Total	

55

Nature pie charts

Practice

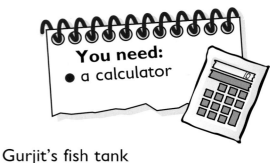
You need:
● a calculator

The pie charts show the fish in three tanks.

Ben's fish tank   Larry's fish tank   Gurjit's fish tank

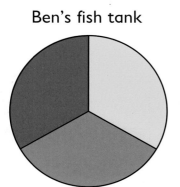 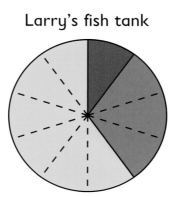 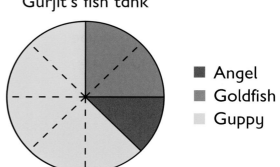

■ Angel
■ Goldfish
□ Guppy

1   Make a table of percentages for each fish tank.

2   a   Whose tank has the greatest percentage of Guppy fish?

    b   Whose tank has the greatest percentage of Goldfish?

    c   Whose tank has the least percentage of Angel fish?

    d   What percentage of Gurjit's fish are Guppy and Angel?

    e   What percentage of Ben's fish are Goldfish and Angel?

    f   Whose fish tank has the most Angel and Guppy fish?

3   The pie chart shows the animals on a farm.

Use your calculator to answer the following questions.
Round your answers to the nearest whole percentage.

    a   Make a table of percentages.

    b   What percentage of the
animals are cows and sheep?

    c   What percentage of the
animals are not sheep?

    d   What is the percentage
difference between chickens
and cows?

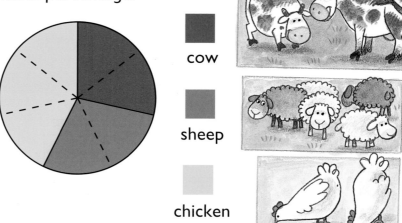

cow

sheep

chicken

Refresher

Animals seen by vet

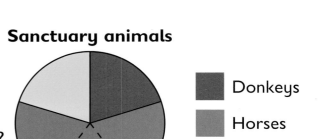

Animal	Percentage
Cats	
Dogs	
Hamsters and Rabbits	
Others	

Legend:
- Cats
- Dogs
- Hamsters & Rabbits
- Others

1 The pie chart shows the animals a vet saw in a week.

   a Copy and complete the table. Do not use your calculator.

   b What percentage of the animals are cats and dogs?

   c What percentage of the animals are hamsters, rabbits and dogs?

   d What percentage of the animals are not dogs?

2 The pie chart shows the animals in a sanctuary.

   a Make a table of percentages.

   b What percentage of the animals are donkeys and horses?

   c What percentage of the animals are not horses?

   d What percentage of the animals are not donkeys or horses?

Sanctuary animals

- Donkeys
- Horses
- Others

Challenge

The pie charts show the birds that visit three gardens.

1 Estimate the percentage of each type of bird. Make a table. Your percentages must add up to 100%.

2 a Which garden has the greatest percentage of blackbirds?

   b Which garden has the smallest percentage of starlings?

Myrna's garden
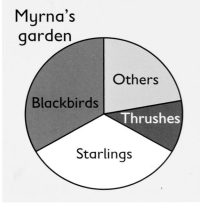

Wayne's garden
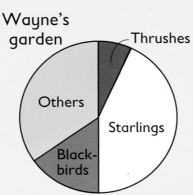

Kim's garden
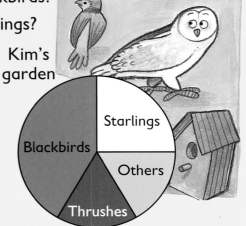

People pie charts

Practice

1 The pie charts show the ages of residents of two hotels.

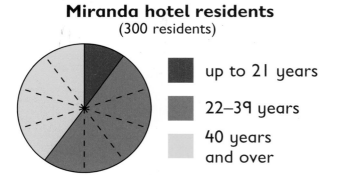

Miranda hotel residents
(300 residents)

■ up to 21 years

■ 22–39 years

□ 40 years and over

Age	Number	Percentage (%)
up to 21		
22–39		
40 and over		

Compton hotel residents
(180 residents)

■ up to 21 years

■ 22–39 years

□ 40 years and over

Age	Number	Percentage (%)
up to 21		
22–39		
40 and over		

a Copy and complete the tables.

b Which do you think is the family hotel? Explain why.

c What percentage of residents staying at the Miranda hotel are over 21 years old?

d What percentage of residents staying at the Compton hotel are under 40 years old?

2 The pie charts show the employees of a bus station and a drinks factory. Make a table for each pie chart.

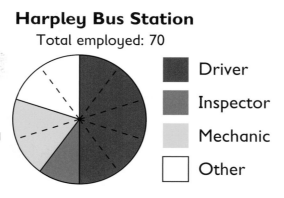

Harpley Bus Station
Total employed: 70

■ Driver

■ Inspector

□ Mechanic

□ Other

Fizz Drinks Company
Total employed: 250

■ Factory

■ Delivery

□ Sales

□ Management

3 The pie chart shows the staff of an airline. There are 24 stewards.

a How many pilots are there?

b How many receptionists are there?

c How many other staff are there?

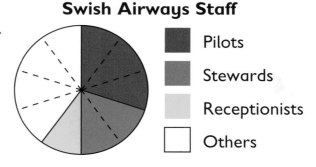

Swish Airways Staff

■ Pilots

■ Stewards

□ Receptionists

□ Others

Refresher

The pie charts show the sizes of families in two districts. Copy and complete the tables.

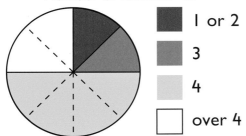

Templeton Estate
Number of families: 48

- ■ 1 or 2
- ■ 3
- ■ 4
- □ over 4

Size of family	Number
1 or 2	
3	
4	
over 4	

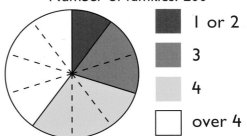

Sidbury Grange
Number of families: 200

- ■ 1 or 2
- ■ 3
- ■ 4
- □ over 4

Size of family	Number
1 or 2	
3	
4	
over 4	

Challenge

You need:
- compasses

1 The table shows the ages of cricket club members.

Draw a pie chart for the table.
Colour the sectors and make a key.

Heathley Cricket Club

Age	Percentage (%)
Under 20	20
20–39	30
40–59	40
60 and over	10

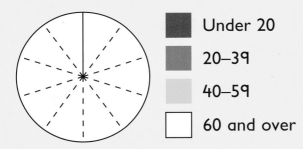

- ■ Under 20
- ■ 20–39
- ■ 40–59
- □ 60 and over

2 Draw pie charts for these tables.

Binkford Bowling Club

Age	Percentage (%)
Under 20	30
20–39	40
40–59	15
60 and over	15

Smallbridge Chess Club

Age	Percentage (%)
Under 20	15
20–39	30
40–59	25
60 and over	30

Experiment percentages

Practice

Work in pairs.

You need:
● a set of dominoes
● a calculator

1 Shuffle the dominoes and lay them face down.
   Choose a domino each.
   Add the dots of both dominoes.
   Do this forty times.

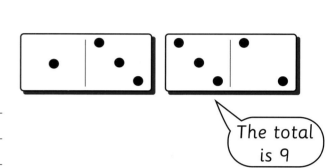

The total is 11

The total is 9

2 Record your results in this tally chart.
   Before you begin, predict which class
   will have the most tally marks.

Total	Tally	Frequency	Percentage
0–4			
5–9			
10–14			
15–19			
20–24			
Total frequency			

3 a Calculate the total frequency.
   b Convert the frequencies to
      percentages.
      Use your calculator.
      Round your answers to the
      nearest whole number.

4 a What is the modal class?
   b What percentage of totals are less
      than 10?
   c What percentage of totals are 15 or more?
   d What percentage of totals lie between 10
      and 19?

5 Make another tally chart.
   This time, record the product of the two
   numbers on each domino. Do this forty times.

6 a What is the modal class?
   b What percentage of products are less than 15?
   c What percentage of products are 20 or more?

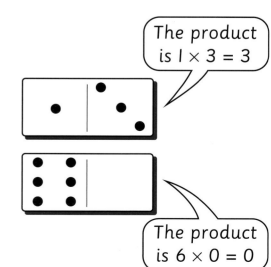

The product is 1 × 3 = 3

The product is 6 × 0 = 0

Refresher

You need:
- two 1–6 dice
- a calculator

Example

$2 \times 3 = 6$

Work in pairs.

1   Take turns to roll the dice. Add 1 to each number.
Find the product of these numbers. Do this 30 times.

2   Record your results in this tally chart.
Before you begin, predict which class
will have the most tally marks.

3   a   Calculate the total frequency.
   b   Convert the frequencies to
      percentages.
      Use your calculator.
      Round your answers to the
      nearest whole number.

4   What is the modal class?

Product	Tally	Frequency	Percentage
0–9			
10–19			
20–29			
30–39			
40–49			
Total			

Challenge

You need:
- five 1–6 dice
- a calculator

Total is 15

Work in pairs.

1   Take turns to roll the dice.
Add the numbers together.
Do this 30 times.

2   Make a tally chart for your results.
Decide the classes you will need.
Before you begin, predict the
modal class.

3   Convert the frequencies to
percentages.

4   a   What is the modal class?
   b   What percentage of totals are
      less than 20?
   c   What percentage of totals are 10 or more?

Total	Tally	Frequency	Percentage
Total frequency			

61

Percentage bar charts

Practice

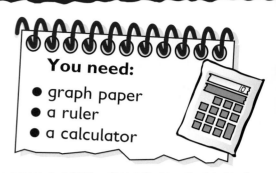

You need:
● graph paper
● a ruler
● a calculator

The numbers show the ages of people when they passed their driving tests.

Ken 22	Brian 21	Jamil 26	Pam 20	Jason 53	Harold 18	Dave 19
Peggy 18	Terri 42	Meera 18	Paula 21	Chin Lin 37	Harry 18	Tim 54
Beth 20	Sandra 17	Phillip 20	Janine 48	Peter 47	Frances 74	Liz 36
William 21	Cassi 30	Sven 51	Ann 25	Walter 33	Emma 36	Joan 66
Mary 18	Val 23	Alex 25	Rafik 17	Ryan 19	Gus 23	Neil 18
Simon 42	Terri 47	Liam 31	Leon 62	Karim 46	Dean 51	Holly 64
Olive 49	Tammy 17	Kevin 19	Nathan 44	Ben 38	Archie 25	
Josy 18	Jez 22	Carrie 50	Iris 53	Sheila 20	Tom 21	

1   Copy the tally chart. Which do you think will be the modal class? Why?

Age	Tally	Frequency	Percentage
10–19			
20–29			
30–39			
40–49			
50–59			
60–69			
70–79			
Total frequency			

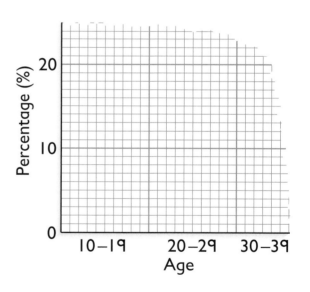

2   Record the data in your tally chart.

3   Calculate the total frequency.

4   Convert the frequencies to percentages.
    Use your calculator. Round the percentages to the nearest whole number.

5   a   What percentage passed their test aged less than 30?
    b   What percentage passed their test aged above 49?
    c   What percentage passed their test aged between 30 and 49?
    d   Estimate the percentage that passed their test aged less than 25.

6   Copy and complete the percentage bar chart.

Refresher

The numbers show how many times 40 people have been abroad in the last five years.

14	1	12	5	6	17	23	5	0	2	23	17	5	1	9	10	0	6	1	14
15	12	1	18	4	0	5	9	0	4	14	6	2	29	7	3	28	1	5	4

1 Copy the tally chart. Which do you think will be the modal class? Why?

Times abroad	Tally	Total
0–4		
5–9		
10–14		
15–19		
20–24		
25–29		

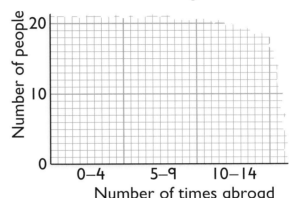

2 Record the data in your tally chart.

3 a How many people went abroad less than 15 times?

  b How many people went abroad at least 20 times?

  c How many people went abroad 10 to 19 times?

4 Copy and complete the bar chart.

Challenge

These bar charts show how long adults and children took to complete a puzzle.

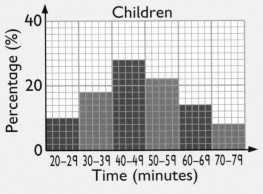

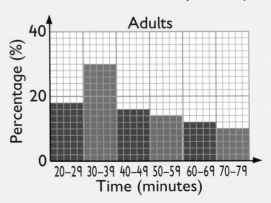

  a Who do you think did best overall: children or adults?

  b Compare the percentage of adults and children who took an hour or more.

Results pie and bar charts

Practice

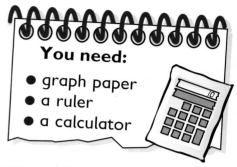

You need:
● graph paper
● a ruler
● a calculator

80 children in Year 6 took a **science** test. The test was out of 25 marks. The pie chart shows their results.

Science test results

■ 1–5
☐ 6–10
▨ 11–15
▨ 16–20
▨ 21–25

Total children = 80

Score	Number of children	Percentage
1–5		
6–10		
11–15		
16–20		
21–25		
Total		

1 Copy and complete the table.

2 **a** What percentage of the children scored less than 11 marks?
  b What percentage of the children scored 11 or more marks?
  c What percentage of the children scored between 11 and 20 marks?
  d What percentage of the children scored between 6 and 15 marks?
  e What is the modal class?

3 Copy and complete this bar chart.

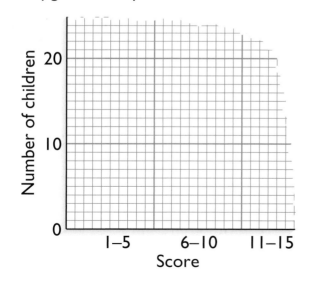

4 This pie chart shows the **history** results for Year 6.
  a Make a table like the one above.
  b Write three sentences comparing the science and history results.

History test results

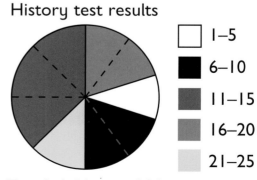

☐ 1–5
■ 6–10
▨ 11–15
▨ 16–20
▨ 21–25

Total children = 240

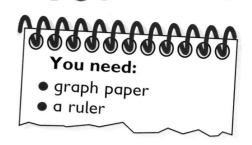

You need:
- graph paper
- a ruler

Refresher

Gary played a computer game lots of times.
The pie chart shows his scores.

Gary's results

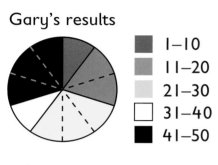

- 1–10
- 11–20
- 21–30
- 31–40
- 41–50

Score	Percentage
1–10	
11–20	
21–30	
31–40	
41–50	
Total	

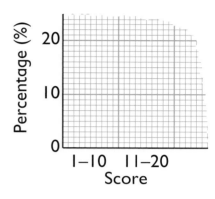

1 Copy the table.

2 a In what percentage of the games did he score above 10?
   b In what percentage of the games did he score below 21?
   c In what percentage of the games did he score above 20?
   d In what percentage of the games did he score between 11 and 30?
   e What is the modal class?

3 Copy and complete the percentage bar chart.

Challenge

You need:
- a calculator
- a ruler

The bar chart shows the runs scored by batsmen
during a cricket tournament.

1 Copy and complete the table.

2 Draw a pie chart to show the scores.

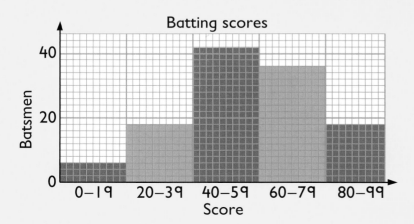

Score	Number of batsmen	Percentage (%)
0–19		
20–39		
40–59		
60–79		
80–99		
Total		

Mirror lines

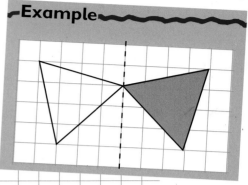

Practice

1 Copy each shape and mirror line onto squared paper.

Use the mirror line to find and draw the reflected shape.

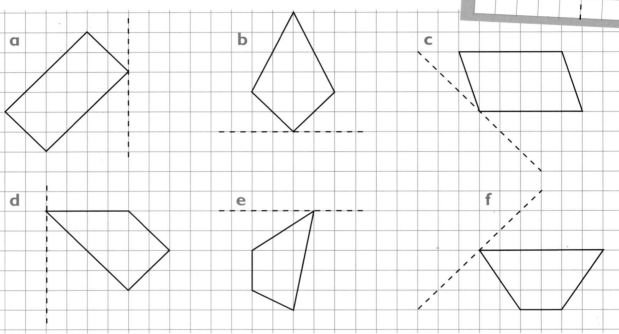

a   b   c

d   e   f

2 Choose materials and draw accurately the reflections of these pentominoes.

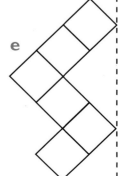

a

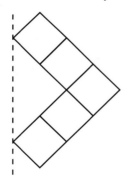

b

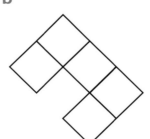

c

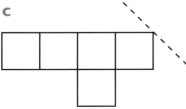

d

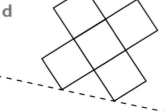

e

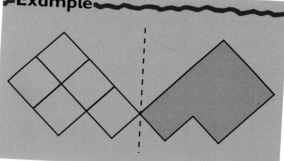

Refresher

Copy these shapes onto squared paper.
Draw the mirror line.
Using the mirror line, find and
draw the reflected shape.

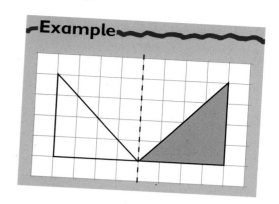

Example

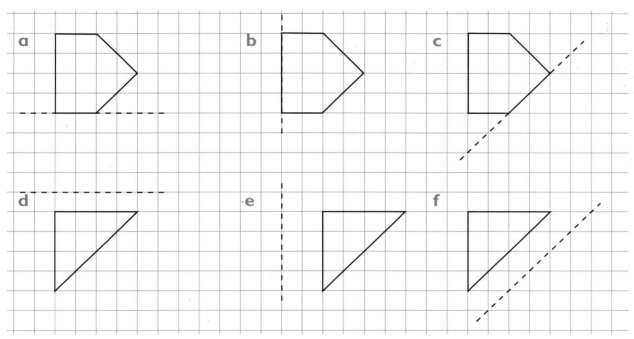

Challenge

1 This is half a shape.
Draw 3 different whole shapes
the original could have been.
Mark the lines of symmetry.

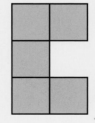

2 Do the same for these half shapes.

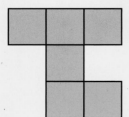 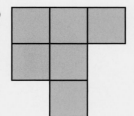 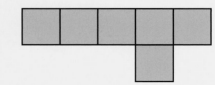

More mirror lines

Practice

Work with a partner.

You need:
- interlocking equilateral triangle tiles
- a mirror
- I cm triangular grid paper
- colouring materials

1 ● Take turns to make the shapes below with the interlocking triangular tiles.
   ● Choose a point and ask your partner to build the reflected shape.
   ● Use the mirror to check.

2 ● Copy the shape and its reflection onto I cm triangular grid paper.
   ● Colour the triangles.

Example

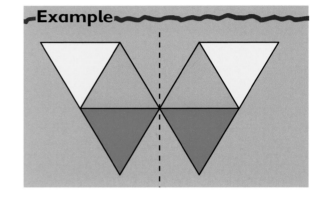

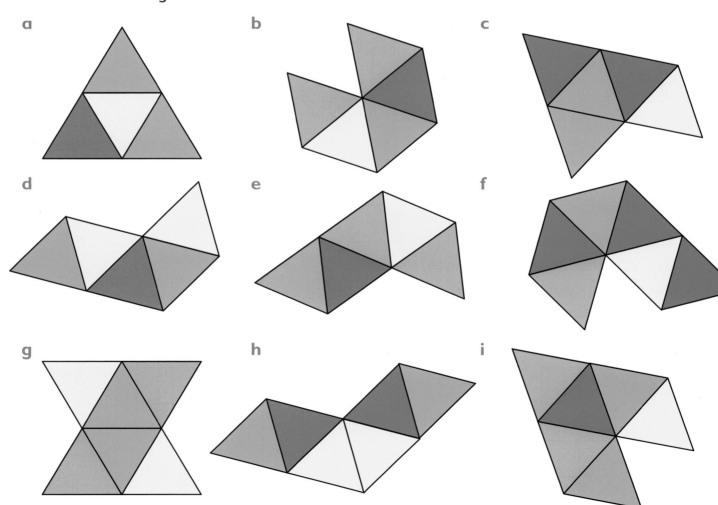

a

b

c

d

e

f

g

h

i

Refresher

Copy these shapes on to 9 × 9 co-ordinate grid paper.
For each shape, the dotted line is the mirror line.

1 a Complete the rectangle ABCD.
  b Write the co-ordinates of B and C.

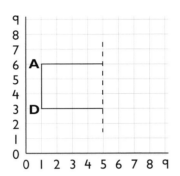

2 a Complete the rectangle PQRS.
  b Write the co-ordinates of Q and R.

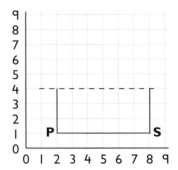

3 a Complete the square EFGH.
  b Write the co-ordinates of F and G.

4 a Complete the isosceles trapezium KLMN.
  b Write the co-ordinates of M and N.

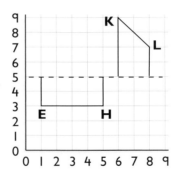

Challenge

You need:
● tracing paper ● 2D shapes

What if ....

a you draw a mirror line across a 2D shape …

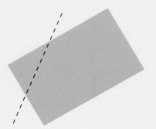

b trace the shape and the mirror line …

c flip the tracing paper and line up the 2 shapes

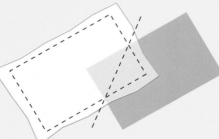

1 Investigate this technique for:
  a the same shape with different positions for the mirror line.
  b different shapes where the mirror line is drawn across the shape.

Four quadrant reflection

Practice

Use a different grid on your Resource Copymaster 17 of 4 quadrant co-ordinate grid paper for each question.

In each grid, the x-axis and y-axis are mirror lines.

Reflect each shape first in the y-axis, then reflect both shapes in the x-axis.

Example

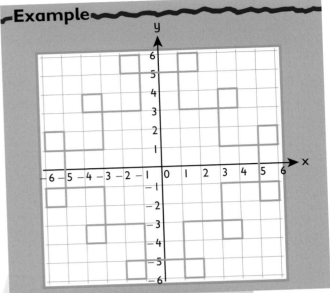

a
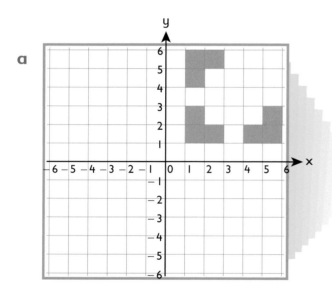

b
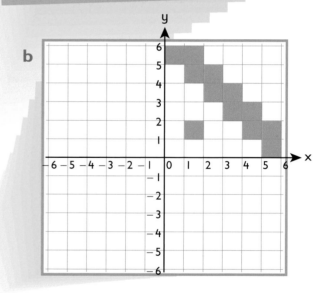

c
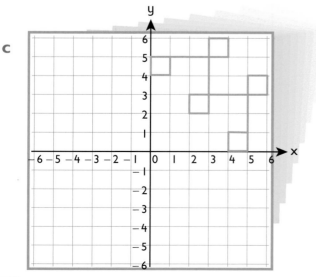

d
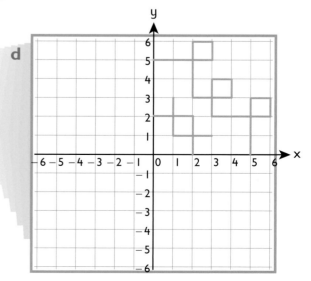

Refresher

The y-axis is the mirror line for each of these shapes.

1 Copy each shape onto squared paper.
Label the axes.

2 Reflect each shape into the 2nd quadrant.

3 For each shape write down the co-ordinates
for points of the reflected rectangle.

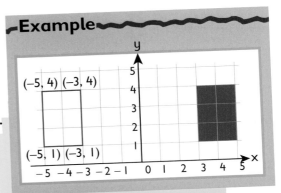

a

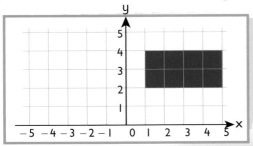

b

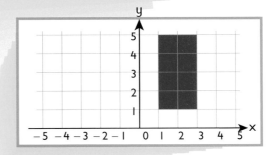

c

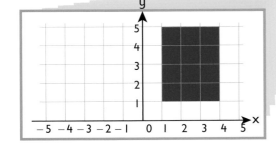

d

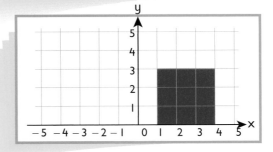

Challenge

The x-axis and the y-axis are the mirror lines for
this star shape.

1 Copy the shape on to co-ordinate grid paper.

2 Copy and complete this table to show the
co-ordinates of
points B, C and D
reflected into all
4 quadrants.

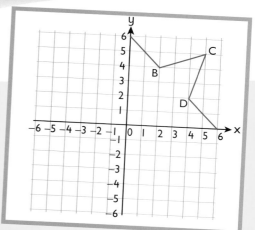

1st quadrant	2nd quadrant	3rd quadrant	4th quadrant
B = (4, 2)	$B_1 =$	$B_2 =$	$B_3 =$
C =	$C_1 =$	$C_2 =$	$C_3 =$
D =	$D_1 =$	$D_2 =$	$D_3 =$

71

Reflecting flags

You need:
- a sheet of 3×3 square grid paper
- felt-tip pens in blue, yellow and red

Practice

1 On your sheet of 3×3 square grids, draw the different flags which can be made with 3 blue squares and 6 yellow squares.

Remember

Rotations of the same design are not allowed

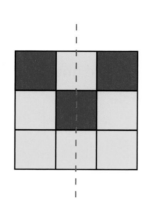 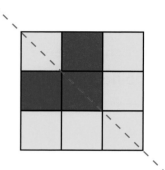

2 Use your red pen to mark the lines of symmetry on each flag. Here are two ways:

3 How many different flags can you make which have 4 blue squares and 5 yellow squares?

4 What if you had 5 blue squares and 4 yellow squares? How many different flags can you make?

5 Copy and complete the table below.

Number of blue squares	Number of flags
1	3
2	6
3	
4	
5	
6	
7	
8	

Refresher

You need:
- a sheet of 3×3 square grid paper
- felt-tip pens in blue, yellow and red

You can make a flag with 1 blue and 8 yellow squares in three different ways.

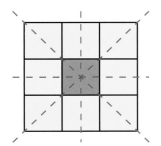 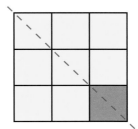 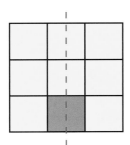

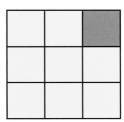

Rotations of the same design are not allowed.

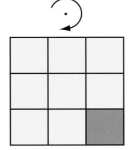

1 Using a sheet of 3×3 square grid paper, find as many different flags as you can which have 2 blue and 7 yellow squares.

2 Mark the lines of symmetry in each flag with dotted red lines.

Challenge

Three-colour flags

How many different four square flags can you make using only 3 colours?

You need:
- a sheet of 2×2 square grid paper
- felt-tip pens in three colours

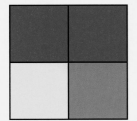 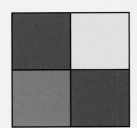 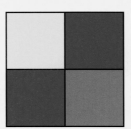

Hint
- Begin with, say, 2 blue, 1 yellow and 1 green square and find all the different flags.
- Rotations of the same design are allowed.

Can you think of a quick way to find all the possible combinations of colours?

Half-turn tessellations

Practice

You need:
- card
- ruler
- sticky tape
- scissors ● A4 paper
- colouring materials

1 Copy and complete Steps 1 to 4.

Step 1
mark midpoints

Draw a quadrilateral.

Measure and mark the midpoint of each side.

Cut out the quadrilateral.

Step 2
modify the shape
and rotate

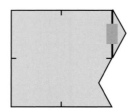

Cut out a shape from the bottom half of one side.

Use the midpoint as a centre of rotation. Turn the shape through 180° and tape it to the top half of the side.

Step 3
modify and rotate

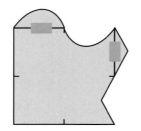

Draw and cut out a curved shape on half of the side.

As before, rotate the piece about the midpoint and tape it to the other half of the same side.

Step 4
modify and rotate

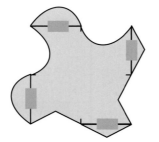

Repeat Step 3 for the other two sides.

New shape

2 Translate your new shape in all directions to make a tessellating pattern.

3 Decorate your design in an interesting way.

You need:
- card
- scissors
- regular hexagon for template
- sticky tape
- circle or coin
- colouring material

Refresher

1 Follow these steps to make your shape.

Step 1
modify

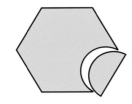

Make a regular hexagon out of card.

Use the coin to draw a semi-circle.

Cut out the semi-circle.

Step 2
translate

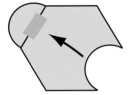

Slide the semi-circle to the opposite side of the hexagon.

Tape the straight edges.

Step 3
modify and translate

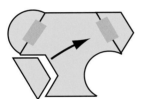

Cut out a trapezium shape like this.

Slide it across the hexagon.

Tape it to the opposite side.

Step 4
modify and translate

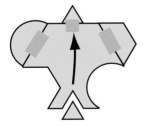

Repeat Step 3 for this triangle.

2 Make a repeating pattern with your new shape. Decorate your tiles.

Challenge

Investigate the "cut and slide" techniques with squares.
Modify by rotating a whole side about a corner and 2 half-sides about the midpoint.

Make repeating patterns and decorate your shapes in an interesting way.

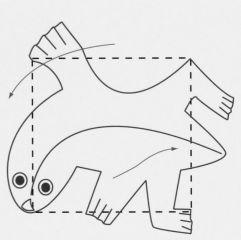

Translating designs

Practice

1   Take your square of card and cut out a simple shape from one or two edges of the card.

Here are some ideas to help you.

2   Draw the net of a cube which has sides of 4 cm.

3   Transfer your design to each face of the cube so that the design will translate round the four sides.

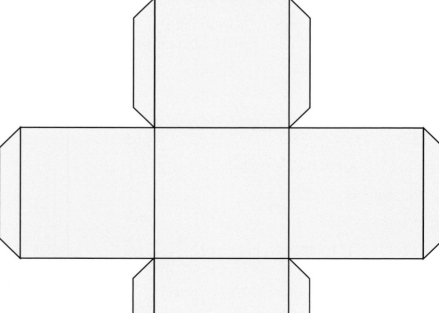

4   Cut out your cube and fold it up.

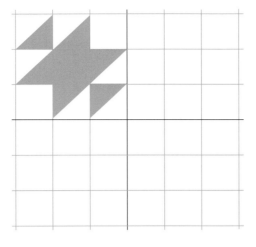

Refresher

1 Mark out a 6 cm × 6 cm square like this.

Join the mid points.

You now have 4 middle-sized squares, each divided up into 9 small squares.

You need:
- a half sheet of 1 cm squared paper
- ruler
- colouring materials

2 Copy the above tile pattern on to the first middle-sized square.

Complete the translating pattern for all 4 squares. Colour your design.

3 Draw another 6 cm × 6 cm square and mark it out in the same way.

Design your own pattern and translate it into all four squares.

Challenge

This is a Navajo blanket design, known as the "Eye Dazzler".

You need:
- triangular dot paper
- ruler
- colouring materials

1 Copy the design on to 1 cm triangular dot paper.

2 Translate the design 4 times.

You might want to begin like this.

77

Rotating patterns

Practice

For each shape, write the number of times it will fit into its outline in one whole turn.

a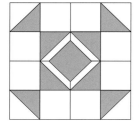

b

c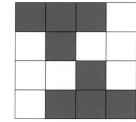

d

e

f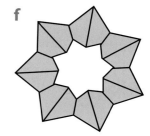

g

h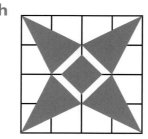

i

j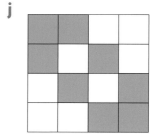

k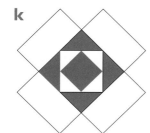

l

m

Refresher

You need two hexagonal shaped triangular grids like this and some colouring materials.

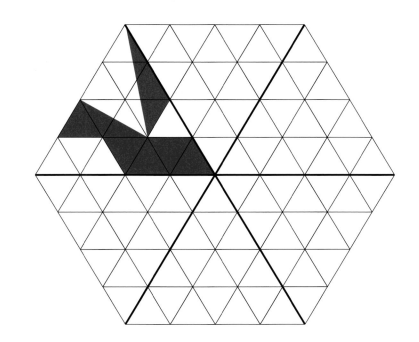

1 a Copy the shape onto your hexagonal grid paper.

   b Rotate the shape into the other 5 triangles.

   c Use colour to highlight the rotating pattern.

2 Use another hexagonal grid. Draw your own rotating design in all 6 triangles.
Colour your design.

You need:
- 1 cm triangular grid paper
- glue
- scissors
- colouring material
- backing paper

Challenge

Draw different half side rotating patterns where the starting shape is a rhombus or a parallelogram.

Stick your rotating pattern onto backing paper and colour your design.

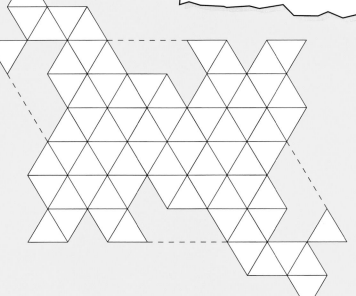

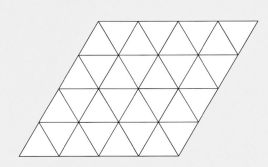

79

Rotating designs

Practice

1 Draw a circle with a radius of 5 cm and construct a basic "hex" pattern.

Draw all lines lightly, some will be erased later.

Follow these steps to make your design.

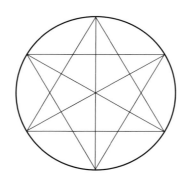

You need:
● compasses
● a ruler
● a sharp pencil
● colouring materials

Erase the circle . . .

draw a hex pattern inside the first . . .

erase some lines.

Finish with this design . . .

or this one.

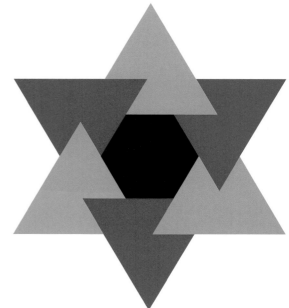

2 Colour your pattern to make a rotating shape.

3 Start with a basic "hex" pattern and make your own rotating design.

Refresher

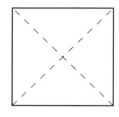

You need:
- two squares of card
- ruler
- compasses
- colouring material

1 a Find the centre of each square by drawing in the diagonals.

20 cm   10 cm

b Draw a circle with a radius of 5 cm.
Divide the circle into 30° sectors.

c Line up the vertex of the smaller square with a radius. Draw around the square lightly in pencil.

d Rotate the square until the vertex lines up with the next radius. Draw round the square.
Repeat once more for the small square.

2 Repeat **1b–d** for the larger square.
Colour your pattern.

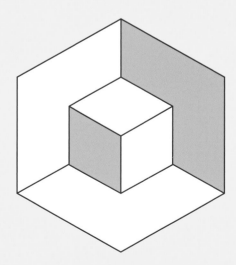

Challenge

Using the basic "hex" pattern, find a way to construct these designs.

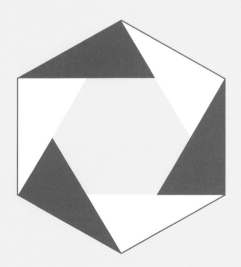

Intersecting lines

New Homes
in Silverknowes Estate

Every house is:
- on one side of a straight road
- at an equal distance from its neighbour

Straight lines of underground pipes connect each house to:
- the Gas works
- the Water Tower

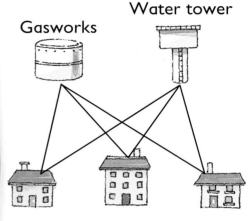

In this diagram there are 3 houses and 3 intersections where the gas and water pipes cross over.

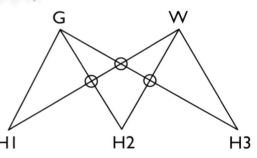

1 a How many intersections are there for a road of 4 houses?
   Copy this diagram.
   b What if there are 5 houses? 6 houses? 7 houses?
   Draw diagrams to help you.

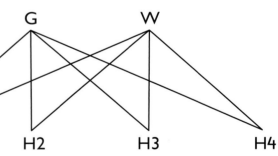

2 Copy and complete this table.

Number of houses	Number of intersections
2	
3	3
4	
5	
6	
7	

3 Predict the number of intersections for a road of 10 houses.

You need:
● Resource Copymaster 22
● ruler

Refresher

Use your Resource Copymaster.

Complete the two mystic rose patterns.

Draw straight lines to join each dot to every other dot.

a 10-dot mystic rose

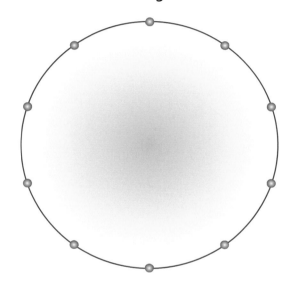

b 12-dot mystic rose

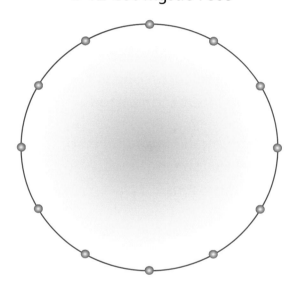

Challenge

Connecting flights

This diagram shows connecting UK flights for 5 airports.
You can fly from one airport to any other airport.
You have a choice of 10 connecting routes.

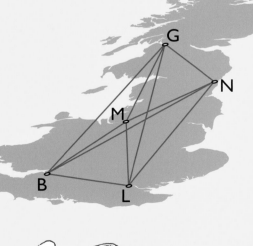

How many connecting flights are there for 8 airports? 10 airports?
Any number of airports worldwide?

Cuts and pieces

Practice

The Post Office is listing post codes
for a new estate.

If the estate has 2 roads then it has
4 post codes for each part of a road.

If there are 3 roads, crossing like this,
then the maximum number of post
codes is 9 because each road is cut
into 3 parts by intersecting roads.

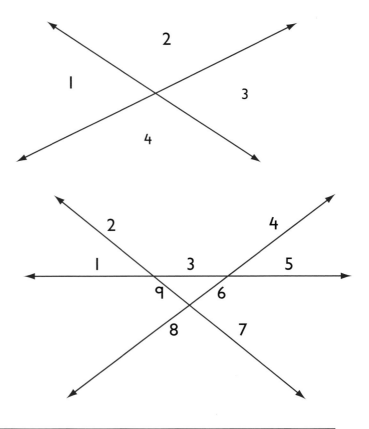

1 What is the maximum number of
   post codes for an estate with
   6 intersecting roads?

2 a Enter your results in a table.
   b Discover the patterns.
   c Use the patterns to
      complete the table.

a Number of intersecting roads	b Number of intersection points	c Total number of post codes needed
2	1	4
3	3	9
4		
5		
6		
7		
8		
9		
10		

3 Name the sequence of numbers in column **b** and in column **c**.

Refresher

These pizzas have been cut into slices in different ways:

1 straight cut
2 slices

2 straight cuts
3 slices   4 slices

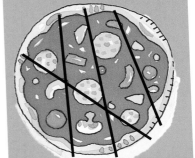

Example

4 straight cuts

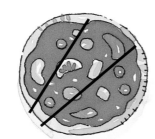 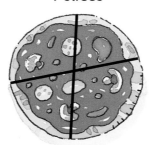 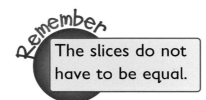

1 Draw some circles for pizzas.

Using only 4 straight cuts across each time, find and draw ways to cut the pizza into 5 slices, 6 slices, 7 slices, 8 slices, 9 slices, 10 slices and 11 slices.

Remember

The slices do not have to be equal.

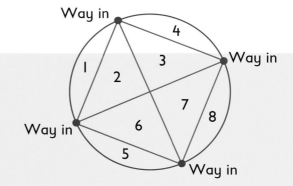

Way in

Way in

Way in

Way in

1 2 3 4 5 6 7 8

Challenge

Fontana Park Competition

We have a very large circular flower bed in the centre of the park. Today it has 4 entry points for paths which cut across the flower bed making smaller regions for planting.

Competition Rules

Design a circular flower bed which will give the maximum amount of regions when there are 6 entry points.

All competition entries must have clearly drawn and numbered regions.

Hint: Draw a circle and mark 6 points on the circumference.

Timing problems

Practice

A restaurant chef uses these roasting times for meat and poultry.

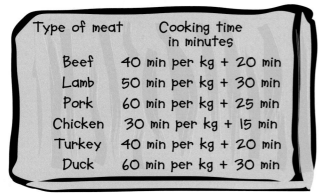

Type of meat	Cooking time in minutes
Beef	40 min per kg + 20 min
Lamb	50 min per kg + 30 min
Pork	60 min per kg + 25 min
Chicken	30 min per kg + 15 min
Turkey	40 min per kg + 20 min
Duck	60 min per kg + 30 min

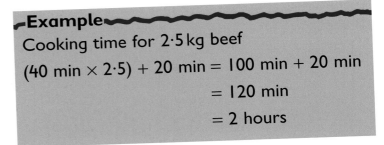

Example
Cooking time for 2·5 kg beef
(40 min × 2·5) + 20 min = 100 min + 20 min
= 120 min
= 2 hours

1 Find the cooking time in minutes, then in hours and minutes for these:

a beef 4 kg

b lamb 3·5 kg

c pork 3 kg

d chicken 2·5 kg

e turkey 4 kg

f duck 2·5 kg

2 The restaurant carvery opens at 5:00 p.m. Work out when the chef must put these meats into the ovens so that they are ready to serve at 5:00 p.m.

Copy and complete this table.

Type of meat	Weight of meat	Roasting time in oven in minutes	Time meat is put into oven
Beef	6 kg		
Lamb	5 kg		
Pork	4·5 kg		
Chicken	5 kg		
Turkey	6 kg		
Duck	4 kg		

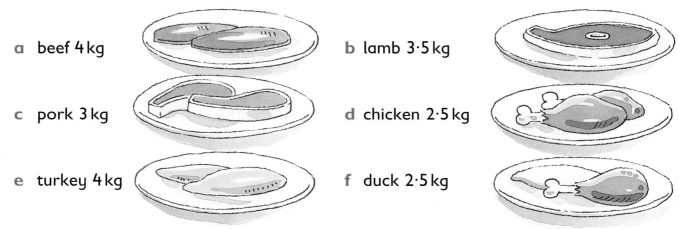

Refresher

1 Copy and complete this table of cooking times.

Cooking time in minutes	Weight in kilograms						
	0·5	1	1·5	2	2·5	3	3·5
Lamb	30	60					
Chicken	20	40					

Roasting times

Lamb
  30 minutes for every 0·5 kg

Chicken
  20 minutes for every 0·5 kg

2 Jean is roasting a 2·5 kg chicken. She puts it into the oven at 4:00 p.m. At what time will the chicken be ready to eat?

3 Robbie roasted a rack of lamb in his oven. It took 2 hours to cook. What weight of lamb did he roast?

Challenge

The chef drew up this "ready reckoner" for roasting beef.

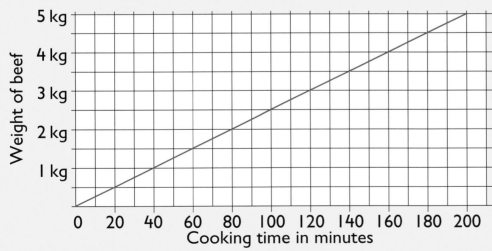

(add 20 minutes to end of cooking time)

Using the graph he worked out that 3 kg of beef needed 120 minutes plus 20 minutes, or 2 hours 20 minutes to cook.

1 Draw up similar graphs for the other meats on the previous page.

2 Use the graph to work out the cooking time for 3 kg weights of each meat.

Remember to add the extra minutes to the end of the cooking time.

87

Measuring capacity

Practice

1 Copy and complete the table.

Litres	Millilitres	Centilitres
1·5 l	1500 ml	150 cl
2·25 l		
3·6 l		
	3260 ml	
	5080 ml	
		75 cl
		105 cl

2 The labels show how much tea each teapot holds when full.

A   B   C   D

4125 ml $3\frac{1}{4}$ l   3·24 l   6·5 l

a Write in litres the capacity of:

(i) teapots A + C   (ii) teapots A + B   (iii) teapots A + D?

b What is the difference in capacity between:

(i) teapots B and C   (ii) teapots B and D?

c How much more tea does pot D hold than pot A?

d Which teapot holds twice as much as pot B?

e What is 3 times the capacity of teapot A in litres?

f If teapot C is half full, how many centilitres of tea does it hold?

g $\frac{2}{5}$ of the tea in pot B are poured out. How many millilitres of tea does the pot still contain?

Refresher

1 Copy and complete

1 litre = ☐ ml

1 litre = ☐ cl

1 centilitre = ☐ ml

Example

10 ml = 1 cl

2 Write these in centilitres.

   a 50 ml   **b** 500 ml   **c** 750 ml   **d** 1000 ml

   e 80 ml   **f** 90 ml   **g** 440 ml   **h** 2000 ml

3 Write these in millilitres.

   a 10 cl   **b** 100 cl   **c** 25 cl   **d** 5 cl

   e 37 cl   **f** 98 cl   **g** 400 cl   **h** 4 cl

Challenge

At the end of the party for Year 6 there were 5 partially full bottles of lemonade.

1 Use this information to list the 5 bottles in order of capacity, largest first.

   A holds more than **B**.

   C does not hold the least.

   A does not hold the most.

   E holds more than **C**.

   Only one bottle holds less than **D**.

   Two bottles hold more than **C**.

2 The measured amounts of lemonade in each bottle are:

   100 cl, 75 cl, 50 cl, 25 cl and 10 cl.

   Work out how much lemonade is in each bottle A to E.

Litres and millilitres

Practice

1 Convert these litres to millilitres, then to centilitres.

a $2 \cdot 5 l$

b $2 \cdot 25 l$

c $2 \cdot 050 l$

d $0 \cdot 52 l$

e $5 \cdot 02 l$

f $25 \cdot 0 l$

2 Write these millilitres as centilitres, then as litres.

a $7650 \, ml$

b $560 \, ml$

c $20 \, ml$

d $5070 \, ml$

e $700 \, ml$

f $70 \, ml$

3 Copy and complete.

a

Amount	Rounded to nearest	
	$\frac{1}{10}$ litre	litre
$2 \cdot 25 l$	$2 \cdot 3 l$	$2 l$
$3 \cdot 706 l$		
$6 \cdot 088 l$		
$7 \cdot 990 l$		

b

Amount	Rounded to nearest	
	$\frac{1}{10}$ litre	litre
$530 \, ml$	$0 \cdot 5 l$	$1 l$
$818 \, ml$		
$4420 ml$		
$690 \, ml$		

4 Work out the answers to these in two ways.
Write your answer in millilitres.

a $\frac{1}{4}$ of $2 \cdot 4 l$

b $\frac{1}{5}$ of $4 \cdot 0 l$

c $\frac{1}{2}$ of $7 \cdot 6 l$

d $\frac{1}{3}$ of $5 \cdot 7 l$

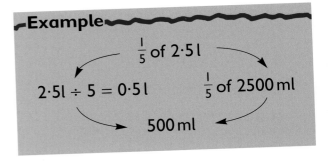

Example

$\frac{1}{5}$ of $2 \cdot 5 l$

$2 \cdot 5 l \div 5 = 0 \cdot 5 l$

$\frac{1}{5}$ of $2500 \, ml$

$500 \, ml$

5 Write true or false for each of these statements.

a $\frac{1}{2}$ of $3 l > \frac{1}{4}$ of $5 l$

b $\frac{1}{2}$ of $1 \cdot 5 l < \frac{1}{4}$ of $2 l$

c $\frac{3}{4}$ of $1 l > \frac{2}{3}$ of $900 \, ml$

d $\frac{1}{4}$ of $1 l < \frac{1}{5}$ of $750 \, ml$

e $\frac{1}{3}$ of $1 \cdot 8 l > \frac{3}{4}$ of $1200 \, ml$

f $\frac{4}{5}$ of $2 l < \frac{2}{5}$ of $5000 \, ml$

Refresher

Example
6143 ml
Answer: 6000 ml

1 Write the number of millilitres shown by the bold figure 6.

a 2146 ml   b 3·6 l   c 4·166 l

d 3·16 l   e 6·462 l   f 6045 ml

2 Find and write the pairs of matching capacities.

Example
250 ml = 0·25 l

$\frac{3}{4}$ litre

0·8 l

5·6 l

800 ml

3·4 l

0·6 l

5600 ml

0·75 l

0·3 l

300 ml

3400 ml

600 ml

Challenge

Copy and complete these patterns as far as you can go.

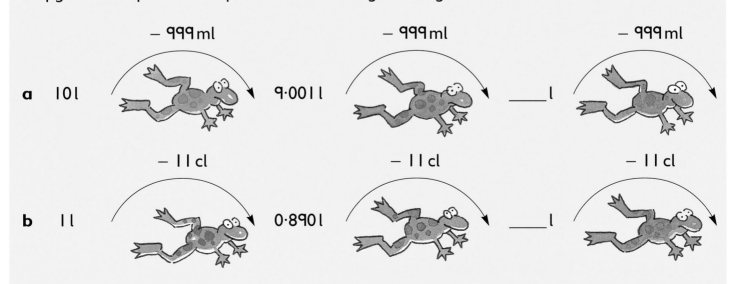

a 10 l   − 999 ml   9·001 l   − 999 ml   ____ l   − 999 ml

b 1 l   − 11 cl   0·890 l   − 11 cl   ____ l   − 11 cl

91

Litres, pints and gallons

Practice

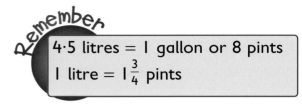

Remember

4·5 litres = 1 gallon or 8 pints
1 litre = $1\frac{3}{4}$ pints

You will find this scale beside the
petrol pumps in filling stations and garages.
Use the scale to answer these questions.

1 Write your answer to the nearest litre.

Approximately how many litres are there in:

a 2 gallons   b 3 gallons   c 4 gallons

d 8 gallons   e 0·9 gallons   f 1·8 gallons?

2 Write your answer to one decimal place.

Approximately how many gallons are there in:

a 7 litres   b 10 litres   c 14 litres

d 45 litres   e 22 litres   f 27 litres?

3 A milkman has 120 houses on his round.

He delivers 1 pint of milk to $\frac{1}{4}$ of the houses

and 2 pints to $\frac{1}{2}$ of the houses.

The rest of his customers take 3 pints of milk.

Work out the quantity of milk he delivers each day:

a in pints
b in gallons
c in litres

4 The milkman's order for
the local primary school is
45 litres of milk per week.

How many pints of milk
does the milkman deliver to
the school each day?

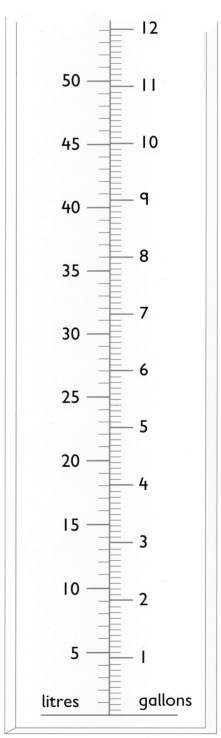

litres   gallons

Refresher

Use the graph to answer these questions.

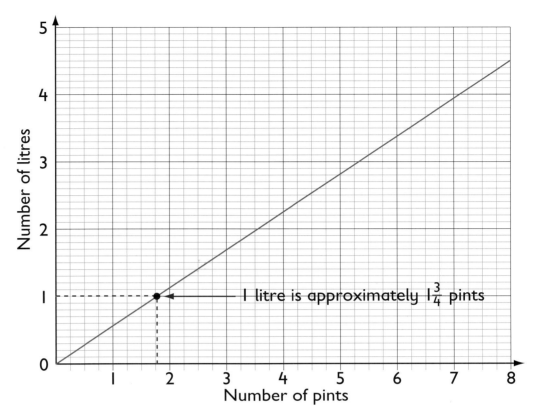

Number of litres

I litre is approximately 1¾ pints

Number of pints

1   Approximately how many pints are there in:

    a   4 litres   b $4\frac{1}{2}$ litres   c $2\frac{1}{2}$ litres   d   2 litres?

2   Approximately how many litres and tenths of a litre are there in:

    a   I pint   b $2\frac{1}{2}$ pints   c $6\frac{1}{4}$ pints   d   8 pints?

Challenge

The petrol tank capacities for these super minis are:

Fiat Punto   10·3 gallons

Ford Fiesta   8·8 gallons

Rover 25   11·0 gallons

Toyota Yaris 9·7 gallons

VW Polo   9·8 gallons

Using the scale on the previous page, work out how many litres, to the nearest litre, there are in a full tank of petrol for each car.

Marine centre problems

Practice

Kevin's job is to refuel the boats.

He completes these columns in his record book for each sale.

Name of boat	Meter reading in litres		
	before refuelling	after refuelling	litres sold
Sea Hawk	7326 l	7430 l	104 l
Sea Urchin	7430 l	7665 l	
Sea Eagle	7665 l		269 l
Sea Farer		8481 l	547 l

1   Work out the missing lines in Kevin's record book for the Sea Urchin, Sea Eagle and Sea Farer.

2   The ferry to the island has two fuel tanks.

   a   How much fuel altogether is in the ferry's tanks?

   b   How much more fuel is in tank 1 than tank 2?

   c   The captain draws alongside to refuel. The ferry needs 4500 litres altogether for the day's ferry crossings.

   Work out how many litres of fuel are added to Tank 1 and Tank 2 so that each tank holds the same amount.

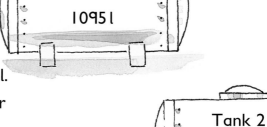

Tank 1
1095 l

Tank 2
876 l

3   The large marine aquarium is stocked with 25 fish, each fish having approximately 18 litres of water. What is the capacity, in litres, of the aquarium?

Refresher

A goldfish needs 9 litres of water.

1 Work out how many goldfish you can keep in tanks which have these capacities.

   a 90 litres   b   45 litres

   c 108 litres   d   450 litres

2 You want to stock some tanks with goldfish. Work out the capacity of the tank you need for these numbers of goldfish.

   a 4 goldfish   b   8 goldfish

   c 20 goldfish d   100 goldfish

Example

27 litres in tank.

Number of goldfish $= 27 \div 9$

$= 3$ goldfish

Example

1 goldfish needs 9 litres

For 6 goldfish $= (6 \times 9)$ litres

$= 54$ litres

Challenge

> For water
>
> $1\,ml = 1\,g$
>
> $1000\,ml = 1000\,g$.

The training pool for young children holds 80 000 litres of water.

1 Using the table, find the weight of water in the pool.

2 Chemicals are added to the water in the pool at regular intervals.

If 500 ml of chemicals are needed for every 10 000 litres, how many litres of chemicals have to be added to the water?

Vertically adding

Example

```
  89 631
  56 333
 145 964
```

Practice

1 Make up 20 addition calculations using these numbers.

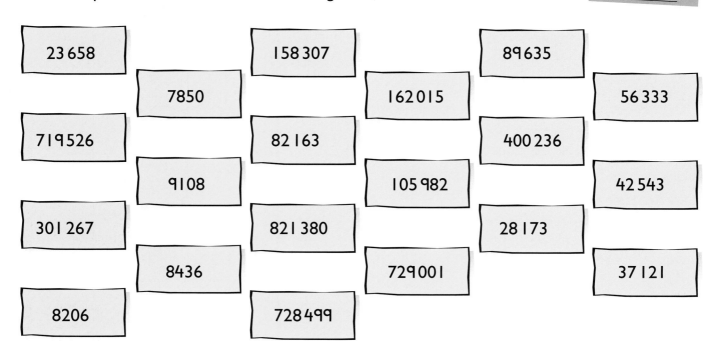

23 658	158 307		89 635
	7850	162 015	56 333
719 526	82 163	400 236	
	9108	105 982	42 543
301 267	821 380	28 173	
	8436	729 001	37 121
8206	728 499		

2 Make up 20 more addition calculations using these numbers.

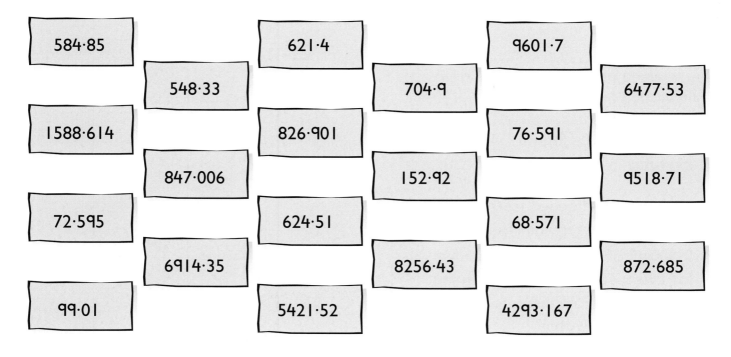

584·85	621·4	9601·7	
	548·33	704·9	6477·53
1588·614	826·901	76·591	
	847·006	152·92	9518·71
72·595	624·51	68·571	
	6914·35	8256·43	872·685
99·01	5421·52	4293·167	

Refresher

Addition facts to 20

1 Write the answers to these calculations as quickly as you can.

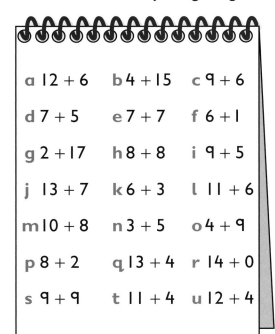

a 12 + 6   b 4 + 15   c 9 + 6

d 7 + 5   e 7 + 7   f 6 + 1

g 2 + 17   h 8 + 8   i 9 + 5

j 13 + 7   k 6 + 3   l 11 + 6

m 10 + 8   n 3 + 5   o 4 + 9

p 8 + 2   q 13 + 4   r 14 + 0

s 9 + 9   t 11 + 4   u 12 + 4

2 Copy out these calculations vertically and work out the answer.

a 365 + 3921   b 759 + 8541

c 5962 + 4198   d 625 + 384

e 725 + 4593   f 9607 + 831

g 5333 + 6248   h 4930 + 483

i 7306 + 493   j 351·8 + 632·7

k 6914·2 + 485·7   l 6849·26 + 584·21

m 526·1 + 367·8   n 1633·55 + 486·72

o 596·78 + 153·49   p 664·95 + 725·88

Challenge

Using the digits 2, 0, 7, 9, 4, 3 make these totals by adding two numbers together. In each calculation each digit can only be used once.

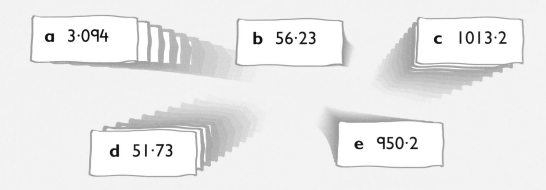

a 3·094

b 56·23

c 1013·2

d 51·73

e 950·2

Vertically subtracting

┌Example┐

2633
− 485
───────
───────

Practice

1 Make up 20 subtraction calculations using these numbers.

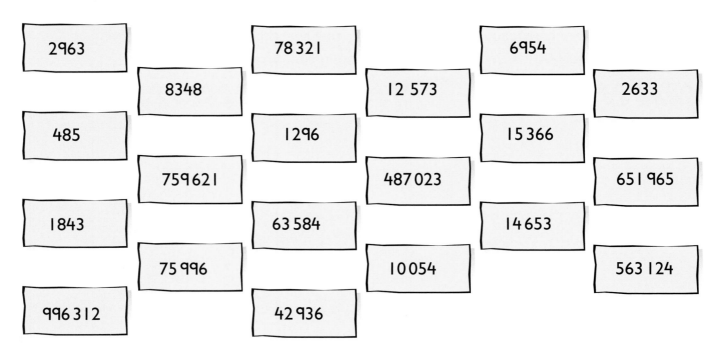

2963	78321	6954
8348	12 573	2633
485	1296	15366
759621	487023	651965
1843	63584	14653
75996	10054	563124
996312	42936	

2 Make up 20 more subtraction calculations using these numbers.

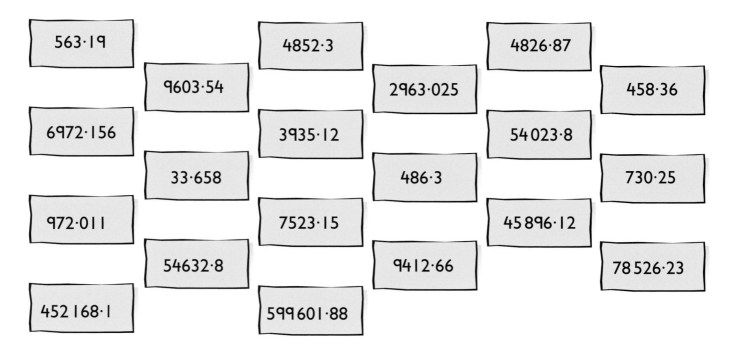

563·19	4852·3	4826·87
9603·54	2963·025	458·36
6972·156	3935·12	54023·8
33·658	486·3	730·25
972·011	7523·15	45896·12
54632·8	9412·66	78526·23
452168·1	599601·88	

Refresher

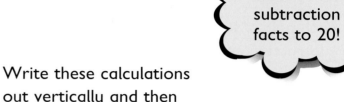

You must learn all the subtraction facts to 20!

Subtraction facts to 20

1 Write the answers to these subtraction calculations as quickly as you can.

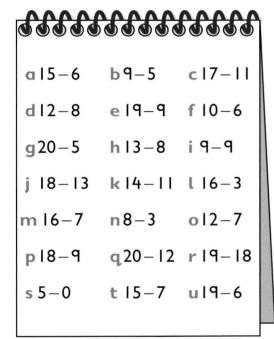

a 15−6 b 9−5 c 17−11

d 12−8 e 19−9 f 10−6

g 20−5 h 13−8 i 9−9

j 18−13 k 14−11 l 16−3

m 16−7 n 8−3 o 12−7

p 18−9 q 20−12 r 19−18

s 5−0 t 15−7 u 19−6

2 Write these calculations out vertically and then work out the answer.

a 4835−1256   b 842−351

c 7802−3657   d 19 873−523

e 14 932−7521   f 6388−921

g 71 952−825   h 77 604−15 402

i 95 317−4526   j 782·3−51·9

k 485·12−96·43   l 455·9−122·4

m 6933·5−42·8   n 78·56−24·99

o 653·56−81·59   p 6214·87−591·06

Challenge

Using the digits 1, 2, 3, 4, 5, 6 make these totals by subtracting two numbers together. In each calculation each digit can only be used once.

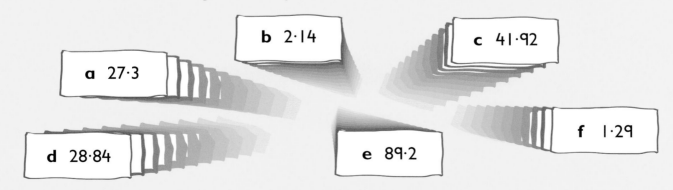

a 27·3

b 2·14

c 41·92

d 28·84

e 89·2

f 1·29

Sums and differences

Practice

Using each pair of two-digit numbers, make an addition and a subtraction calculation. Then write out any other calculations that you could use the answers to work out.

Example

51, 67

$51 + 67 = 118$

$67 - 51 = 16$

I can work out the answers to these calculations:

$510 + 670 = 1180$

$6.7 - 5.1 = 1.6$

$0.51 + 0.67 = 1.18$

$6700 - 5100 = 1600$

and there are more!

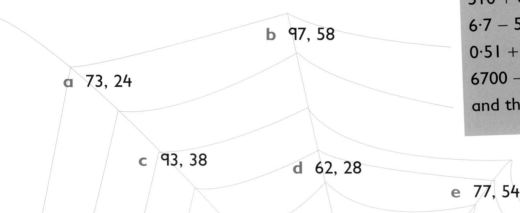

b 97, 58

a 73, 24

c 93, 38

d 62, 28

e 77, 54

i 86, 49

f 61, 38

g 99, 87

h 14, 67

j 83, 49

k 19, 89

l 51, 17

m 59, 47

n 25, 92

o 47, 88

r 29, 39

p 42, 91

q 37, 55

s 96, 29

t 84, 21

Refresher

1 Work out these calculations in your head.

a 49+27

b 37+84

c 71+21

d 93+44

e 58+32

f 76+47

g 29+19

h 37+73

i 26+67

j 82+37

k 86−31

l 74−29

m 95−36

n 78−49

o 66−23

p 71−59

q 97−48

r 63−14

s 55−27

t 88−41

Now choose two of the calculations and explain in words how you worked them out.

2 Work out the first calculation and then use the answer to work out the following calculations.

a 59 + 26
590 + 260
5900 + 2600

b 48 + 21
480 + 210
4800 + 2100

c 72 + 68
720 + 680
7200 + 6800

d 57 + 29
570 + 290
5700 + 2900

e 88 + 51
880 + 510
8800 + 5100

f 62 + 91
620 + 910
6200 + 9100

g 91 − 35
910 − 350
9100 − 3500

h 74 − 18
740 − 180
7400 − 1800

i 52 − 31
520 − 310
5200 − 3100

j 69 − 48
690 − 480
6900 − 4800

k 37 − 12
370 − 120
3700 − 1200

Challenge

Design a game that involves adding and subtracting two-digit numbers.
Make it as fun as you can!

Sums and differences 2

Practice

Copy the calculations and work out the missing numbers.

a 50 + 30 + 80 + ▢ = 200

b ▢ + 70 + 10 + 50 = 170

c 90 + 50 + 60 + ▢ = 260

d 40 + ▢ + 70 + 50 = 220

e 60 + 80 + ▢ + 70 = 240

f 50 + ▢ + 90 + 80 = 230

g ▢ + 90 + 20 + 30 = 210

h 20 + 60 + 80 + ▢ = 240

i 30 + ▢ + 30 + 90 = 210

j 50 + ▢ + 40 + 10 = 150

k 80 + 70 + ▢ + 50 = 260

l ▢ + 80 + 70 + 10 = 220

m 50 + 40 + 30 + ▢ = 190

n 56 + ▢ + 31 + 47 = 226

o 63 + 97 + ▢ + 62 = 273

p 72 + ▢ + 46 + 29 = 162

q ▢ + 64 + 71 + 52 = 286

r 28 + 49 + 72 + ▢ = 182

s ▢ + 66 + 17 + 38 = 170

t 67 + 38 + ▢ + 88 = 212

u 49 + 37 + 19 + ▢ = 160

v 72 + ▢ + 81 + 69 = 259

w 49 + 67 + ▢ + 39 = 183

x 82 + 91 + ▢ + 37 = 256

y 19 + ▢ + 46 + 47 = 194

2 Find the pairs of numbers that equal 0·1.

0·08   0·06   0·09   2·7

0·02

0·07   9·6

0·3   0·4   0·04   5·5   1·2

0·05

0·2   0·5   0·01

0·1   2·1   7·9

0·7   0·05   6·3

0·9   8·8   3·7

0·5   0·6   0·03   0·4   4·5

0·8   7·3

1 Find the pairs of numbers that equal 1.

3 Find the pairs of numbers that equal 10.

Challenge

Work out these calculations using brackets and multiplication.

Example
32 + 38 + 31 + 30
I can work this out as:
$(30 \times 4) + 2 + 8 + 1$

a 59 + 52 + 51 + 50

b 71 + 73 + 76 + 78

c 66 + 60 + 64 + 69

d 20 + 21 + 22 + 23

e 81 + 89 + 83 + 87

f 39 + 33 + 31 + 35

g 16 + 14 + 18 + 10

h 43 + 44 + 49 + 48

i 99 + 96 + 91 + 93

j 25 + 26 + 27 + 28

Problem solving

Practice

Work out the answers to these problems.
Choose the method of working you are going to use.
Explain **why** you chose that method.

1 5 friends are going shopping. In total they
   spend £51·15. What was the average amount spent?

2 The most popular book at the book shop costs £6·75. In one week the shop
   sells 1849 copies. How much money do they take?

3 I have counted the cars in the supermarket car park. There are 85 red cars,
   65 silver cars, 92 blue cars and 77 black ones. If each car had four passengers,
   how many people at the supermarket came by car?

4 The theme park keeps a record of the number of visitors each day. In a week
   (Monday to Friday) 15 363 people visited. The figures for Monday to
   Thursday are:

   Monday   2680
   Tuesday   3463
   Wednesday   1097
   Thursday   2155

   How many people visited on Friday?

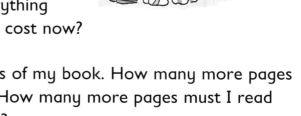

5 I want a coat priced £68·50 and some shoes
   priced £28·98. The shop reduces everything
   by half. How much will the two items cost now?

6 I have read 83 pages of the 644 pages of my book. How many more pages
   must I read before I finish my book? How many more pages must I read
   before I reach the middle of the book?

Refresher

1   I want to buy a new shirt for £19·43. I have £11·02 so far. How much more do I need?

2   My ticket to go into the cinema cost £6·50 and my drink and ice cream cost £3·82. How much did I spend altogether?

3   We picked 97 apples from our tree. We gave 49 to the next door neighbours. How many did we have left?

4   I have saved £30·72 but my sister has saved £7·58 more than me. How much does she have?

5   My mum is trying to save £1000. She has £792. How much more does she need to reach her target?

6   There are 305 children in the assembly sitting on the floor and there are 126 sitting on chairs. 56 of the children leave the hall. How many are left?

Challenge

Make up 4 problems for your friend.
Use the following information and add more in of your own if you need to.

You are going on holiday to Spain.
The flight costs £89.
There are 270 pesetas to the pound.
It takes 2 hours 45 minutes to fly there.
The hotel costs £24 a night.

Number sequences

Practice

1 Add 0·5 to each of these.

a 0·5	b 0·2
c 1·5	d 0·6
e 2·0	f 6·5
g 3·4	h 5·2
i 0·9	j 12·0

2 Add 0·2 to these.

a 0·2	b 1·0
c 0·5	d 1·3
e 0·8	f 0·6
g 0·1	h 1·7
i 6·5	j 9·0

3 Add 0·25 to these.

a 0·25	b 0·5
c 2·25	d 1·0
e 4·0	f 0·75
g 2·0	h 0
i 3·75	j 5·5

4 Find your way through the maze by adding the number for each footstep.

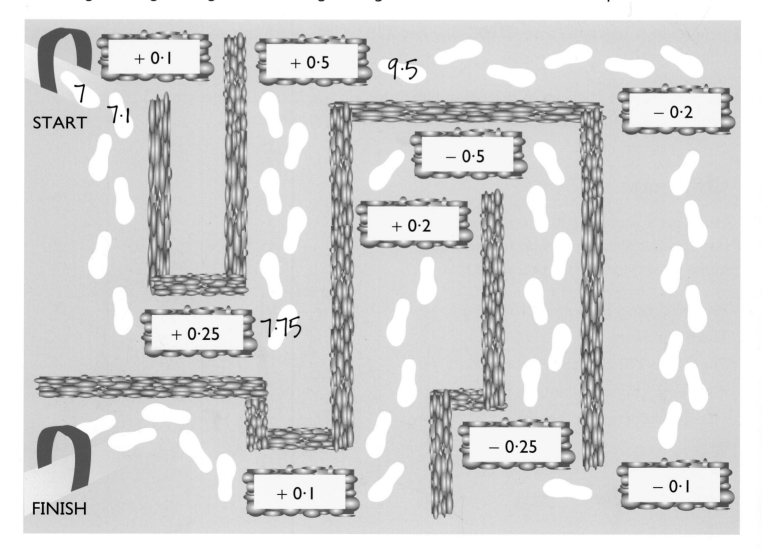

Refresher

Write the next 10 numbers in each of these sequences using the rule shown.

a **The rule is:**
Add 0·2 each time.

1,   1·2,   1·4, ...
+ 0·2   + 0·2   + 0·2

b **The rule is:**
Add 0·1 each time.

6·5, 6·6, ...
+ 0·1   + 0·1

c **The rule is:**
Add 0·5 each time.

7·5, 8·0, ...
+ 0·5   + 0·5

d **The rule is:**
Add 0·25 each time.

3·5, 3·75, ...
+ 0·25   + 0·25

e **The rule is:**
Subtract 0·5 each time.

10·5, 10·0, ...
− 0·5   − 0·5

f **The rule is:**
Subtract 0·25 each time.

9·5,   9·25 . . . .
− 0·25 − 0·25

Challenge

3

27

·7

·03

·25

·15

·5

62

·40

38

What to do

- Choose a different starting number each time.
- Make 10 jumps.
- Jump forwards in steps of
  0·2   0·5   0·1   0·25
  as far as you can.
- Jump backwards in steps of
  0·5   0·1   0·25   0·2
  as far as you can.
- Record each number sequence.

Prime numbers

Practice

1 Every number is the product of prime numbers,
for example: $12 = 2 \times 2 \times 3$

Use a factor tree to find which prime numbers
form each product.

Example

2 and 3 are the prime
factors of 12.

a [18]   b [20]   c [42]

d [30]   e [25]   f [28]

g [32]   h [72]   i [54]

2 Build 3 different factor trees for each
of these numbers.

a [40]   b [24]   c [64]

3 Build 4 different factor trees for each
of these numbers.

a [48]   b [100]   c [36]

4 Look closely at the factor trees you have made for the numbers in Questions 2 and 3.

a Explain why the factor trees are different for the same numbers.

b What is the same about the factor trees for the same
numbers?   Why?

5 Build factor trees for these numbers.

a [15]   b [33]   c [45]   d [21]   e What do you notice?

Refresher

Sort these numbers into 2 groups.

| PRIME | and | COMPOSITE |

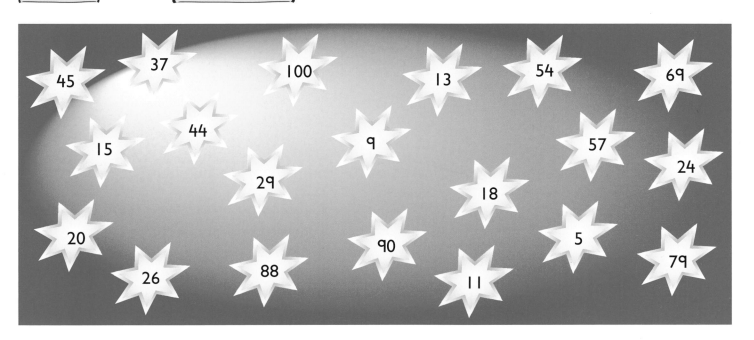

Challenge

Prime numbers to 100 are easy to find!

1   How many prime numbers are there between 100 and 200?
    Make a list.

2   Are there more prime numbers between 1 and 100 or 100 and 200?

3   Are they the same numbers with just 100 added on?

1	2	3	4	5	6	7	8	9	10
11	12	13	14	15	16	17	18	19	20
21	22	23	24	25	26	27	28	29	30
31	32	33	34	35	36	37	38	39	40
41	42	43	44	45	46	47	48	49	50
51	52	53	54	55	56	57	58	59	60
61	62	63	64	65	66	67	68	69	70
71	72	73	74	75	76	77	78	79	80
81	82	83	84	85	86	87	88	89	90
91	92	93	94	95	96	97	98	99	100

Goldbach's conjecture

Practice

Conjecture: n & v

1 An opinion formed based on incomplete information.

2 An opinion or conclusion reached through incomplete information.

Christian Goldbach (1690–1764) was a Professor of Mathematics at the Russian Imperial Academy.

He made the conjecture that:

> Every even number greater than 4 is the sum of two prime numbers.

1 List the even numbers from 6 up to 50.

2 Can each of these numbers be expressed as the sum of 2 prime numbers?

$6 = 3 + 3$

$8 = 3 + 5$

$10 = 3 + 7, 5 + 5$

$12 = . . . , .$

$14 = . . . , ...$

3 Do some of the even numbers have more than one solution?

4 Which number has the greatest collection of pairs of prime numbers that make its total?

5 Can you find any even number that is not the sum of 2 prime numbers?

Try out random even numbers up to 100. Does Goldbach's conjecture work? What about random numbers up to 200?

Refresher

The children in year 6 carried out an *investigation*

All prime numbers occur as pairs of odd numbers

Here are some of their results

5   7
11   13
17   19
29   31

Can you find any other pairs of consecutive odd numbers up to 100 that are prime numbers?

Challenge

Why did Goldbach not include **odd** numbers in his conjecture?

Is every odd number the sum of 2 prime numbers?

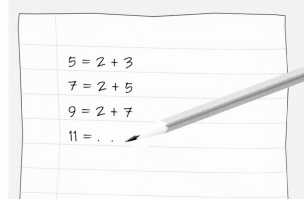

5 = 2 + 3
7 = 2 + 5
9 = 2 + 7
11 = . . .

1   Make a list of odd numbers from 5 up to 49.

2   Can every odd number be expressed as the sum of 2 prime numbers?

3   What do you notice?

Number equations

Practice

1 Balance these equations so both sides of the scales are equal.

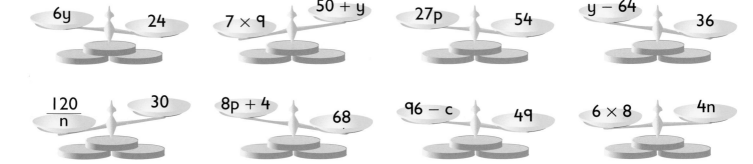

2 Find the solution to these equations.

a $25p = 239 - 139$

b $72 + n = 200 - 56$

c $163 - y = 11^2$

d $157 + 89 = 300 - n$

e $36 \times 3 = 12y$

f $42y = 200 - 32$

g $20\% \times n = 11 \times 3$

h $p + 49 = 7 \times 9$

i $y - 144 = 12^2$

j $50\% \times 126 = \frac{1}{4} \times y$

k $760 \div 10 = 227 - p$

l $84 \times 5 = (6 \times 7)y$

m $25n = 50 \times 24$

n $1001 - 635 = 61p$

3 Write an equation using the letter n to represent the unknown number for each of these statements.

Example
25 more than a number is 100 → $n + 25 = 100$

a 100 less than a number is 25

b 60 times a number is 180

c a number increased by 27 is 84

d 44 times 4 is a number

e a number decreased by 52 is 100

4 Find the value of n in the equations in Question 3.

Refresher

Copy and complete.

Find the missing numbers.

1
a $6 \times \boxed{} = 48$
b $27 + \boxed{} = 50$
c $\boxed{} \times 7 = 49$
d $\boxed{} - 56 = 44$
e $2 \times \boxed{} + 10 = 28$
f $36 \div 4 = \boxed{}$

2
a $\frac{1}{2} \times \boxed{} = 327$
b $4 \times \boxed{} = 200$
c $\boxed{}^2 = 144$
d $\boxed{} - 129 = 11$
e $56 \times \boxed{} = 168$
f $95 \div \boxed{} = 19$

3
a $72 \div \boxed{} + 2 = 10$
b $34 \times \boxed{} = 136$
c $\frac{1}{2} \times \boxed{} = 68$
d $57 \times \boxed{} = 5700$
e $\boxed{} \div 10 = 930$
f $\frac{1}{4} \times 600 = \boxed{}$

Challenge

1 How many different equations can you make using all of these cards?

2 Can you find the answer to each of your equations?

3 Add an extra card.    What equations can you make using all of the cards now?

Writing formulas

Practice

I For each sequence:

- Identify the rule
- Write the next 5 numbers in each sequence
- Write the rule
- Devise a formula

a	3, 30, 300 . . .	The rule is . . .	Formula =
b	84, 90, 96 . . .	The rule is . . .	Formula =
c	3, 6, 12 . . .	The rule is . . .	Formula =
d	791, 781, 771 . . .	The rule is . . .	Formula =
e	2, 6, 18 . . .	The rule is . . .	Formula =
f	6, 13, 27 . . .	The rule is . . .	Formula =
g	8192, 4096, 2048 . . .	The rule is . . .	Formula =
h	−250, −275, −300 . . .	The rule is . . .	Formula =
i	0·7, 0·9, 1·1 . . .	The rule is . . .	Formula =

2 The formula is $\boxed{T = n \times c}$ → T = total cost
n = number of items
c = cost per item

Apply the formula to find out the total cost of the number of items shown.
Copy and complete the tables.

a Cost = 12p

n	5	7	12	19	8	25	49	100
T								

b Cost = £22

n	6	9	20	15	11	26	32	50
T								

Refresher

1 Follow the rule. Write the next 5 numbers in each sequence.
Change the rule into a formula.

a The rule is: subtract 5 each time → 650, 645, . . . , . . .
-5 → Formula =

b The rule is: add 25 each time → 375, 400, . . . , . . .
$+25$ → Formula =

c The rule is: multiply by 3 each time → 2 , 6 , . . . , . . .
$\times 3$ → Formula =

d The rule is: divide by 2 each time → 256, . . . , . . .
$\div 2$ → Formula =

e The rule is: double each time → 30, . . . , . . .
$\times 2$ → Formula =

Challenge

Write a rule and a number sequence for each formula below.

Choose a new start number each time for your sequence from the wheel.

| a n + 5 | | b 2n − 1 | | c n × 10 |

| d $\frac{1}{2}$n | | e n − 15 | | f 2n + 2 |

| g 3n | | h 2n + n |

Write 5 numbers in each sequence.

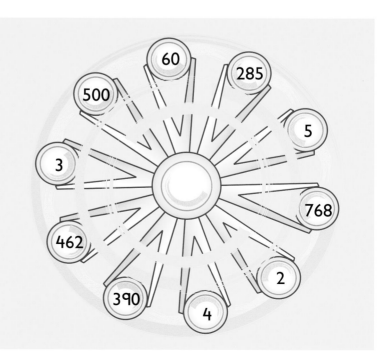

Glossary

angles

right angle

acute angle

obtuse angle

180°　straight line

Angles are formed when two straight lines meet. We measure an **angle** by measuring the amount of turn from one line to the other.

Angles are measured in degrees. The symbol for degrees is °.

A right angle is 90 degrees, 90°. A right angle is shown by a small square.

An acute angle is less than 90°.

An obtuse angle is more than 90°.

A straight line has an angle of 180°. This can be used to work out the second angle.

arc

Any part of the circumference of a circle is called an **arc**.

See also circumference

area

Area is the amount of surface of a shape. It is measured in square centimetres. This can be abbreviated to cm².

You can work out the **area** of a rectangle by multiplying the length of the shape by the breadth. Length × breadth = **area**.

average

The **average** is the middle amount in any range of data.

You calculate the average by adding all the amounts then dividing by the number of items.

Marks in a maths test	
Joe　　42	Average = 42 + 55 + 68 + 59 = 224
Sue　　55	224 ÷ 4 = 56
Helen　68	The average score is 56
Sam　　59	

Mean is another word for **average**.

axis, axes

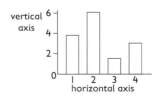

Graphs and charts have two **axes**.

The horizontal **axis** shows the range of data. The vertical **axis** shows the frequency. They can be labelled in any equal divisions.

brackets

Brackets are used in maths for grouping parts of calculations together.

10 − (3 + 4) = 3
(10 − 3) + 4 = 11

The calculations in brackets need to be worked out first.

capacity

Capacity is the *amount* that something will hold.
Capacity is measured in litres and millilitres.
I litre is equal to 1000 millilitres.

Litres can be abbreviated to l.
Millilitres can be abbreviated to ml.

Capacity can also be measured in pints and gallons.

See imperial units

circumference

The **circumference** is the distance all the way round a circle.

column addition

When you add large numbers, using the standard vertical method can make the calculation easier.

The numbers must be written with the digits of the same place value underneath each other.

If the digits in one column add up to more than 9, the tens are carried to the next column.

column subtraction

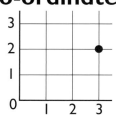

When you subtract large numbers, using the standard vertical method can make the calculation easier.
The numbers must be written with the digits of the same place value underneath each other.

◀ If the top digit is lower than the bottom digit then 10 can be "borrowed" from the next column.

common denominator

A **common denominator** is when two or more fractions have the same denominator.

Fractions with different denominators need to be changed to have a **common denominator** before they can be added or subtracted.

$\frac{1}{2} + \frac{1}{4}$ can be changed to $\frac{2}{4} + \frac{1}{4}$

The **common denominator** is 4.

See also equivalent fractions

concentric

Concentric means *with the same centre*.

These circles are **concentric**.

co-ordinates

Co-ordinates are numbers or letters that help us to plot the exact position of something. We use them on maps, graphs or charts.

◀ Graphs like this are called the first quadrant.
On the graph, the dot is at (3, 2): 3 lines across and 2 lines up.
To read **co-ordinates** we look *across* and *up*. Some people remember this by thinking of "Along the corridor, up the stairs".

decimals

Decimal fractions show us the part of a number that is not a whole number.

The decimal point separates the whole numbers from the decimal fractions.

H	T	U	•	ths	hdths
		5	•	8	
		5	•	8	6

◀ Each digit after the decimal point has a different place value.

5·8 is a number with one decimal place.

5·86 is a number with two decimal places.

Decimals and fractions

All decimals have a fraction equivalent. To find the decimal equivalent for a fraction we divide 1 by the denominator and then multiply by the numerator.

$\frac{3}{4}$ = 0·75

1 ÷ **4** = 0·25

0·25 × **3** = 0·75

$\frac{1}{2}$ = 0·5

$\frac{1}{4}$ = 0·25

$\frac{3}{4}$ = 0·75

$\frac{1}{10}$ = 0·1

$\frac{3}{10}$ = 0·3

$\frac{1}{5}$ = 0·2

$\frac{1}{100}$ = 0·01

$\frac{3}{100}$ = 0·03

See also fractions

dividing by 10, 100 and 1000

When a number is **divided by 10, 100 or 1000** the digits move one, two or three place values to the right. If the hundreds, tens and units digit is zero it disappears; if it is not zero it becomes a decimal.

The place value of the digits decreases 10, 100 or 1000 times.

See also multiplying by 10, 100 and 1000

divisibility

There are some quick tests you can do to see if one number will divide by another.

You can use your knowledge of multiplication facts: 3 × 4 = 12 so 12 is divisible by 3 and 4.

Other tests:

2s   Any even number is divisible by 2.

4s   If you can divide the last two digits of the number by 4 exactly, the whole number will divide exactly by 4. 216 is divisible by 4 as 16 is divisible by 4.

5s	You can divide 5 exactly into any number ending in 5 or 0.
10s	If a number ends in 0 you can divide it by 10 exactly.
100s	If a number ends in two zeros it will divide exactly by 100.
1000s	Any number that ends in three zeros is divisible by 1000.

dodecahedron

A **dodecahedron** is a solid shape with 12 faces.
The faces are pentagons.

equivalent fractions

Equivalent fractions are fractions of equal value. They are worth the same.

$\frac{4}{8}$ is equivalent to $\frac{1}{2}$

See *also* common denominator

See *also* fractions

factor

A **factor** is a whole number which will divide exactly into another whole number.

The factors of 12 are 1, 2, 3, 4, 6, 12 as they all divide into 12.

The factors can be put into pairs. If the pairs are multiplied together they will equal 12.

1 × 12
2 × 6
3 × 4

formula

A **formula** is a way of writing down a rule.

For example, to find the area of a rectangle you multiply the length by the width.

fractions

Fractions are parts of something.

$\frac{1}{2}$ →numerator
→denominator

The numerator tells you how many parts we are talking about.
The denominator tells you how many parts the whole has been split into.

fractions and division

We find fractions of amounts by dividing by the denominator and then multiplying by the numerator.

We divide by the denominator as this is the number of parts the amount needs to be divided into. We then multiply by the numerator as this is the number of parts we are talking about.

See *also* fractions

imperial units	These used to be the standard measurements in Britain. They have now been replaced by metric units. Some imperial units are still used today.

Capacity
1 pint = 0·568 l
8 pints = 1 gallon

Mass
1 ounce (oz) = 28·35 g
1 pound (lb) = 16 ounces

Length
1 yard = 0·914 m
1 mile = 1·6 km
1 inch = 2·54 cm
1 foot = 0·305 m

improper fraction

An **improper fraction** is a fraction where the numerator is more than the denominator.

$\frac{13}{5}$

These are sometimes called "top-heavy" fractions.
Improper fractions can be changed to whole numbers or mixed numbers.

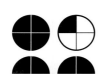

◄ $\frac{5}{4} = 1\frac{1}{4}$

◄ $\frac{8}{4} = 2$

A fraction that is not an **improper fraction** is a proper fraction.

See also fractions

integer

Integer is another name for a whole number.

intersection

If two lines **intersect** they cross each other.

These lines intersect at **A**.
A is the point of intersection.

inverse operations

Inverse means *the opposite operation*. The **inverse operation** will undo the first operation.

Addition and subtraction are **inverse operations**:
17 + 26 = 43   43 − 26 = 17

Multiplication and division are **inverse operations**:
6 × 9 = 54   54 ÷ 9 = 6

length

Length is how long an object or a distance is.
Length is measured in kilometres, metres, centimetres and millimetres.

1 kilometre is equal to 1000 metres.
1 metre is equal to 100 centimetres.
1 centimetre is equal to 10 millimetres.

Kilometre can be abbreviated to km.
Metre can be abbreviated to m.
Centimetre can be abbreviated to cm.
Millimetre can be abbreviated to mm.

Length can also be measured in miles.

See also imperial units

long division

When you divide numbers which are too large to work out mentally, you can use **long division**. We call it **long division** when both numbers involved are two digits or more.

long multiplication

When you multiply numbers which are too large to work out mentally, you can use **long multiplication**. We call it **long multiplication** when both numbers involved are more than a single-digit.

```
      3 5 2
  ×     2 7
  7 0 4 0
  2 4 6 4
  9 5 0 4
      1
```

The numbers must be written with the digits of the same place value underneath each other.

See also short multiplication

mass

Mass is another word for weight.
Mass is measured in grams and kilograms.
1 kilogram is equal to 1000 grams.
Mass can be measured in pounds and ounces.

See also imperial units

mean

Mean is another word for average.

See also average

median

The **median** of a range of data is the item that comes *halfway*.

Marks in a maths test
46   51   52   (60)   62   65   71
60 is the **median**.

mode

The **mode** of a set of data is the number that occurs most often.

multiples

A **multiple** is a number that can be divided into another number.

2, 4, 6, 8, 10, 12 are all **multiples** of 2 as we can divide 2 into them all.

10, 20, 30, 40, 50, 60, 70 are all **multiples** of 10 as we can divide 10 into them all.

Multiples can be recognised by using the multiplication facts.

multiplication

Multiplication is the inverse operation to division.
Numbers can be multiplied in any order and the answer will be the same.
$5 \times 9 = 45$ $9 \times 5 = 45$

See also inverse operations

multiplying by 10, 100 and 1000

Th	H	T	U
		2	3
	2	3	0

$23 \times 10 = 230$

Our number system is based around 10.
When a number is **multiplied by 10, 100 or 1000** the digits move one, two or three place values to the left and zeros go in the empty column to keep its place value.

◄ The place value of the digits increases 10, 100 or 1000 times.

See also dividing by 10, 100 and 1000

negative numbers

Numbers and integers can be positive or **negative**.
Negative integers or numbers are *below* zero.

Negative numbers have a minus sign before them.
-56

Negative numbers are ordered in the same way as positive numbers except they run from right to left.

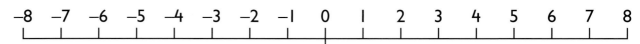

net

A **net** is a flat shape which can be cut out and folded up to make a solid shape.

<, >, ≤, ≥

are symbols used to order numbers.

$<$ means less than $45 < 73$
$>$ means more than $73 > 45$
$\leq$ means less than or equal to $44 \leq 45,\ 44$
$\geq$ means more than or equal to $88 \geq 87,\ 88$

ordering fractions

When you **order fractions** and mixed numbers, first look at the whole numbers then the fractions. If the fractions have different denominators, think about the fractions in relation to a half to help you to order them.

parallel

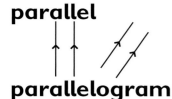

Parallel lines are lines that are the same distance apart all the way along.

◄ They are often shown by two little arrows.

parallelogram

A **parallelogram** is a four-sided shape with its opposite sides parallel to each other.

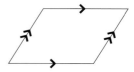

percentage

The sign % stands for *per cent*, which means out of 100.
30% means 30 out of 100.

Percentages are linked to fractions and decimals.
$\frac{1}{2}$ = 50% = 0·5
$\frac{1}{4}$ = 25% = 0·25
$\frac{3}{4}$ = 75% = 0·75
$\frac{1}{5}$ = 20% = 0·2
$\frac{1}{10}$ = 10% = 0·1

Finding percentages of amounts
To find **percentages** of amounts we need to use the relationship to fractions.

To find 50% of an amount, we divide by 2: 50% = $\frac{1}{2}$.
50% of £40 is £20.

To find 25% we divide by 4: 25% = $\frac{1}{4}$
To find 20% we divide by 5: 20% = $\frac{1}{5}$

perimeter

4cm
3cm

perimeter = 3cm + 4cm + 3cm + 4cm = 14cm

Perimeter is the distance all the way around a flat shape.

You can calculate the **perimeter** of a shape by adding the length of all the sides together.

If a shape has sides all the same length then you can use multiplication to work out the **perimeter**.

perpendicular

A **perpendicular** line meets another line at right angles.

pie chart

A **pie chart** is a way of showing information.

Y6 journeys to school

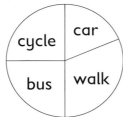

plane

A **plane** is a flat surface.

prime factor   A **prime factor** is a factor which is also a prime number.

See also prime number

See also factor

prime number   **Prime numbers** are numbers that can only be divided by 1 and themselves.

A prime number has only two factors.

17 is a prime number. It can only be divided exactly by 1 and 17.

1 is not counted as a prime number.

The prime numbers to 20 are:

2, 3, 5, 7, 11, 13, 17, 19

probability   **Probability** is about how *likely* or *unlikely* the outcome of an event is. The event may be the throw of a die or whether or not it will rain today.

We use certain words to discuss **probability**. We can put events and the words on a scale from *no chance of it happening* to *certain*.

| impossible no chance | | unlikely | | even chance | | possibly likely | | good chance | | certain |

Even chance means an event is as likely to happen as not happen.

product   **Product** is another name for the answer to a multiplication calculation.

24 is the product of 6 × 4

proportion   **Proportion** shows the relationship between two connected things.

When amounts are being compared and they have equal ratios they are in **proportion**.

1 packet of biscuits costs 60p
2 packets of biscuits cost £1·20
3 packets cost £1·80
The cost is in **proportion** to the number of packets bought.

See also ratio

quadrant   A **quadrant** is a quarter of a circle.

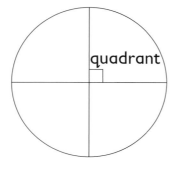

Quadrants are used in graphs.

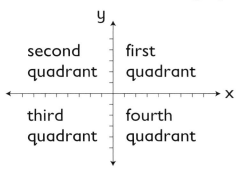

second quadrant	first quadrant
third quadrant	fourth quadrant

quotient

Quotient is another name for the answer to a division calculation.

The remainder of the **quotient** can be shown as a fraction or a decimal fraction.

$27 \div 4 = 6 \text{ r } 3$
$27 \div 4 = 6\frac{3}{4}$
$27 \div 4 = 6\cdot75$

As we are dividing by 4, the fraction will be a quarter and there are 3 of them left. $0\cdot75$ is the decimal equivalent to $\frac{3}{4}$.

range

The **range** of a set of data is the lowest to the highest value.

ratio

Ratio is a way of comparing amounts or numbers.

It can be used in two ways:

It can describe the relationship between *part to whole*.
A cake is divided into 4 equal parts and one part is eaten. The **ratio** of part to whole is one part in every four parts or 1 in 4.

Or it can describe the relationship of *part to other part*.
A cake is divided into 4 parts and one part is eaten. The ratio of part to part is 1 to 3 as for every piece eaten three pieces are left.

The **ratio** 1 to 3 can also be written as 1:3.

See also proportion

reflection

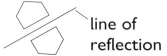
line of reflection

◄ If a shape is **reflected**, it is drawn as it would appear reflected in a mirror held against or alongside one of its sides.

reflective symmetry

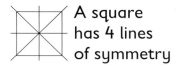
A square has 4 lines of symmetry

A shape is symmetrical if both sides are the same when a line is drawn through the shape. The line can be called a mirror line or an axis.

◄ Some shapes have more than one line of symmetry.

| **rhombus** | A **rhombus** is a four-sided shape. Its sides are all equal in length. The opposite sides are parallel. | 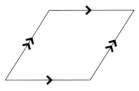 |

round number — A **round number** usually ends in a zero. When using or estimating with large numbers round numbers are easier to work with.

short division — When you divide numbers that are too large to work out mentally, you can use **short division**. We call it **short division** when one of the numbers involved is a single digit.

short multiplication — When you multiply numbers that are too large to work mentally, you can use **short multiplication**. We call it **short multiplication** when one of the numbers involved is a single digit.

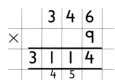

◄ The numbers must be written with the digits of the same place value underneath each other.

See also long multiplication

square numbers — To **square** a number it is multiplied by itself. The answer is a **square number**.

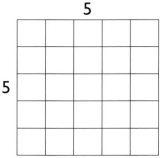

To square 5, we multiply 5 by itself. 25 is the **square number**.

◄ $5 \times 5 = 25$ can also be written as $5^2 = 25$.

Square numbers have an odd number of factors. The factors of 25 are 1, 5, 25.

Square numbers up to 100
$1 \times 1 = 1$
$2 \times 2 = 4$
$3 \times 3 = 9$
$4 \times 4 = 16$
$5 \times 5 = 25$
$6 \times 6 = 36$
$7 \times 7 = 49$
$8 \times 8 = 64$
$9 \times 9 = 81$
$10 \times 10 = 100$

See also factor

symmetrical pattern

Patterns can be **symmetrical**. They may have two lines of symmetry.

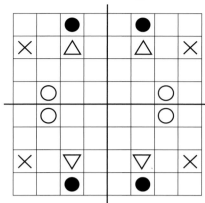

line of symmetry

line of symmetry

time

These are the units **time** is measured in:
seconds
minutes
hours
days
weeks
months
years

These are the relationships between these units:
60 seconds = 1 minute
60 minutes = 1 hour
24 hours = 1 day
7 days = 1 week
4 weeks = 1 month
12 months = 1 year
365 days = 1 year

analogue   digital
clock   clock

◄ **Time** can be read on analogue clocks or digital clocks.

Digital clocks can be 12-hour or 24-hour.
The 12-hour clock uses a.m. and p.m.
The 24-hour clock carries on after 12 o'clock midday to 24 instead of starting at 1 again.

translation

A **translation** is when a shape is moved by sliding it.

trapezium

A **trapezium** is a four-sided shape with two parallel sides.

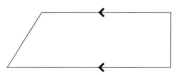

triangles

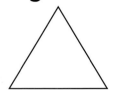

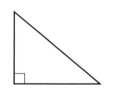

A **triangle** is a 2D shape with three straight sides and three angles.

There are four kinds of triangle:

Equilateral triangle
◄ This has three equal sides and three equal angles.

Isosceles triangle
◄ This has two equal sides. The angles opposite these two sides are also equal.

Scalene triangle
◄ All three sides are different lengths.
The angles are all different too.

Right-angled triangle
◄ This has one right angle.

vertex

The **vertex** is the tip or top of a shape, the point furthest away from the base. The plural is **vertices**.

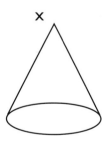

x is the **vertex** of the cone

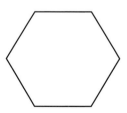

A regular hexagon has 6 vertices